C000186259

through the
German
Waterways

Nautical Canals of Europe series

Philip Bristow

through the German Waterways

NAUTICAL

© Philip Bristow 1988

First published in Great Britain by
Nautical Books
an imprint of A & C Black (Publishers) Ltd
35 Bedford Row, London, WC1R 4JH.

First Hardback Edition published in 1975
© Philip Bristow 1975

ISBN 0 7136 5770 7

By the same author
Bristow's Book of Yachts
Through the French Canals
Through the Dutch and Belgian Canals
Down the Spanish Coast
French Mediterranean Harbours
Round the Italian Coast

Despite every effort to ensure that information given in this book is accurate and up to date, it is regretted that neither author nor publisher can accept responsibility for errors or omissions.

Filmset and printed in Great Britain by
BAS Printers Limited, Wallop, Hampshire

To Emma and Philip

Acknowledgements

I am indebted to many Departments of the German Government for the facts and figures that they have kindly made available to me; to Graf v.d. Schulenburg, Der Bundesminister für Verkehr for particular help and guidance; to many officials in Wasser-und Schiffahrtsdirektion, Fremdenverkehrsverband and Landesverkehrsverband; to Harrad and Archie Swannell for their kindness and help in translation; to Linda Wheeler for unexpected translation help and to my old friend and cousin, Kingsley Horgan, for some expert navigation when it was needed; also to Anthony Hall and Linda Wheeler of Smile Design, Gosport for the artwork.

Contents

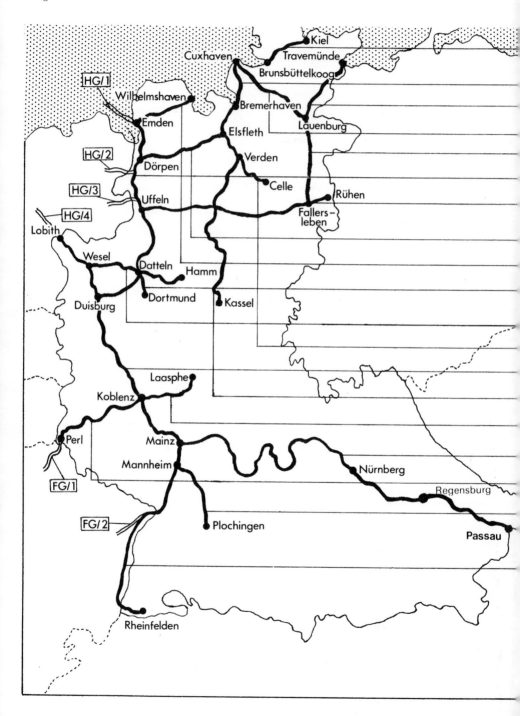

Route 2
Brunsbüttelkoog – Kiel

Route IA
Bremerhaven – Cuxhaven
Route 14
Travemünde – Lauenberg
Route 3
Cuxhaven – Lauenberg
Route 10
Lauenberg – Fallers–leben
Route 6
Emden – Datteln
Route 15
Uffeln – Rühen

Route 5
Elsfleth – Dörpen
Route 18
Wilhelmshaven – Emden
Route 4
Duisburg – Dortmund

Route 17
Wesel – Hamm
Route 1
Bremerhaven – Celle
Route 11
Lobith – Koblenz
Route 16
Verden – Kassel
Route 7
Koblenz – Laasphe

Route 12
Mainz – Nürnberg – Passau (when completed)
Route 9
Koblenz – Perl
Route 13
Mannheim – Plochingen

Route 8
Koblenz – Rheinfelden

1 Summary of Route Details

The Rhine is considered as two routes:—Route 11—From the Dutch border to Koblenz. Route 8 Koblenz to Switzerland.

ROUTE 11	LOBITH to KOBLENZ via Wesel, Düsseldorf, Köln, Bonn Königswinter, Bad Honnef, Remagen, Ehrenbreitsein	River Rhein
ROUTE 12	MAINZ to NÜRNBERG via Frankfurt, Offenbach, Aschaffenberg, Wurtzburg, Bamberg. The Rhine-Main-Danube waterway. (When completed).	River Main, Main-Donnau-Kanal
ROUTE 13	MANNHEIM to PLOCHINGEN via Heidelberg, Heilbronn, Stuttgart	River Neckar
ROUTE 14	TRAVEMÜNDE to LAUENBURG via Lübeck, Molln, Büchen	River Trave, Elbe-Lübeck Kanal
ROUTE 15	UFFELN to RUHEN via Minden, Hannover, Braunschweig	Mittelland Kanal

Summary of Route Details (continued)

ROUTE 16	VERDEN to KASSEL via Hameln, Kassel	River Aller, Mittel-Weser, Ober-Weser, River Fulda
ROUTE 17	WESEL to HAMM via Dorsten, Datteln	Wesel-Datteln-Kanal
ROUTE 18	WILHELMSHAVEN to EMDEN via Aurich	Ems-Jade Kanal

From Holland into Germany

ROUTE HG/1	DELFZIJL to EMDEN	River Ems
ROUTE HG/2	TER APEL to HAREN	Stads Compascuum Kanal Haren-Rüten Kanal, Dortmund-Ems Kanal
ROUTE HG/3	COEVORDEN to LINGEN	Coevorden-Piccardie Kanal, Sud-Nord Kanal, Ems-Vecht Kanal, River Ems
ROUTE HG/4	LOBITH to EMMERICH	River Rhein

From France into Germany

ROUTE FG/1	THIONVILLE to PERL	River Mosel
ROUTE FG/2	STRASBOURG to LAUTERBOURG	River Rhein

2 Cruising Contrasts

Germany is a land of cruising contrasts, displaying concentrated castles and concentrated coal-mines with equal pride and impartiality. You may be pleased as you cruise by forests or pained as you cruise by factories but you will never be bored.

The title of this book would have been more correct before the second world war; today it should read *Through The West German Waterways* or, strictly speaking, *Through The Federal Republic of Germany Waterways* or even *Through Die Bundesrepublik Deutschland Waterways*.

You will find that the terms 'West' and 'East' Germany are avoided in the Federal Republic as is the name German Democratic Republic by which title the Communist countries refer to East Germany.

We go cruising to forget political considerations and newspapers and telephones and bank managers and gas bills and other necessary evils; in mentioning the two Germanys here it is only to explain that this book is concerned with the Federal Republic. Perhaps such an explanation is unnecessary; perhaps you might have assumed that no cruising paradise exists on the 'other side'.

As you will probably know, West Germany is less than half the size of what was pre-war Germany and is now about the size of the United Kingdom with a maximum distance from north to south of about five hundred miles and from east to west of about three hundred. You will see that its borders adjoin Denmark, Holland, Belgium, France, Luxembourg, Austria, Switzerland, Czechoslovakia and East Germany.

On every waterway in West Germany—referred to as Germany from now on—there is interest; on some, you may think, too

... increasing numbers of tourists ... Hamburg.

much. The towns that have been attracting increasing numbers of tourists, Köln, (Cologne), Düsseldorf, Frankfurt, Hamburg, Hannover, Heidelberg, Karlsruhe, Koblenz, Nürnberg, Stuttgart are all on waterways as are, the castles of the Rhine, the castles of the Neckar, the wine festivals of the Rhine and Moselle.

There are busy waterways and peaceful waterways and sections of what must be the most hideously industrialised waterways in the world; yet if, while cruising past the chimneys, you cannot bring yourself to marvel at the achievements of this country in rising from the ashes to be fourth largest steel producer in the world, perhaps you can pass the time by dwelling on a few less smokey German institutions such as Snow White, The Pied Piper, Baron Münchhausen and the Loreley.

Although Germany possesses 4,700 kms of navigable rivers and canals you cannot make as many circular cruises as you can in France, Holland and Belgium. In fact the few available cross the

industrial north and no cruising yacht would wish to endure passing
through such an area at all and yet, would you believe that you
would cruise past a bathing beach in the Ruhr?

Cruising the German Rhine, German Moselle, Main, Neckar
and Lahn all have to be 'there and back again' trips but oddly
enough you discover an advantage in this. If you cruised along
the same waterway twenty times it seems that you are always
passing places that you must stop at next time; 'there and back
again' trips provide this opportunity.

. . . no anchoring by this bathing beach in the Ruhr.

You will have heard how busy German waterways are. An annual movement of hundreds of millions of tons of cargo is not a figure that you can readily translate into terms of barges likely to be encountered as you cruise along. The greatest concentration of inland waterway traffic is in places where you would not wish to linger, the Duisburg-Ruhrort area for instance, which has a big appetite for barge cargoes; so many that you imagine that everything that needs to be carried in Germany is carried by water, but in fact, the percentages are:— Road 42%, Rail 27.8%, Water 25.1%. and Pipeline 5.1%.

Everywhere on every waterway you find efficiency that you are glad to use, of course; but you need to make sure that your leisure attitude does not impede it. The barge you hold up may be one of the 50 per cent of the total fleet who are owner-drivers, aware that just 5 per cent of the fleet who are big business are capturing 56 per cent of the trade.

Threequarters of all cargo moved is now carried in self-propelled craft, which is a good thing if only because it will dispose of some of the long tows that seem to take you about half a day to pass and an interminable time to shepherd in and out of locks. Cargo carried, or pushed, by the big pushers is growing and you would have a job to pass, or to share a lock, with them.

But the first problem for the cruising yachtsman is how to get to Germany.

To those yachtsmen who do not see this as a problem I should mention that many readers of my books have limited experience

. . . Pusher: the new barge power.
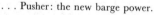

of navigation and seamanship. The majority of long distance crews we have met in the European waterways and the Mediterranean have been made up of man and wife, usually retired and often inexperienced to begin with but managing very well.

I would strongly advise that no inexperienced yachtsman should undertake the open sea passage to the German North Sea ports; even for the experienced yachtsman it can be a very rough ride indeed. You can easily reach the German waterways from Holland or France.

With sufficient seagoing experience it is certainly an interesting exercise to enter Germany through one of her own 'front door' rivers, the Ems, Weser or Elbe. The inland waterway connections with these rivers incidentally, will all be capable of taking the standard 1,350-ton Europaship one day but they are more than adequate for the cruising yacht now.

The North Sea area from the Dutch Ijsselmeer to Denmark is all Friesland and for centuries the Frieslanders have faced a

Towed barges on the Elbe-Lübeck Canal.

battle with the sea. The sea is still battling and in these parts
you certainly need your nautical wits about you. The North Sea
coast of Germany carries on in the same pattern as the
Netherlands with offshore sandy islands or sand dunes; subsidence
and the action of the sea have formed enormous mud banks
known as watten and these are exposed at low tide. The coast is
indented by the estuaries of the rivers already referred to, the
Ems, Weser and Elbe and what are known as the drowned inlets
of the Jade and Dollart Bays.

The sight of these watten or tidal sand flats at low tide is
enough to scare the most slap-happy yachtsman into keeping
strictly to the buoyed channel. From the buoyed channel you see
even the wrecks of CARS that have obviously set out without
tide tables across drying sands and run afloat. At Cuxhaven and
Büsum it is a tourist attraction to ride on horseback or in horse-
drawn coaches to nearby islands.

Only a few of the nearer islands have dry sand approaches at
low tide, the other Frisian islands being connected by ferry,
Borkum from Emden, Juist, Norderney (do you remember
'The Riddle of the Sands'?) and Baltrum from Norddeich,
Langeoog from Bensersiel, Spiekeroog from Neuharlingersiel,
Wangerooge from Wilhelmshaven and Carolinensiel and
Helgoland, (of cheap whisky fame), from Cuxhaven.

At your first sea entry into Germany, to the Ems, you
encounter the shallow flats of Borkum Riff and the island of
Borkum. The river owes its importance to the Dortmund-Ems
canal leading on to the Rhine and the Ruhr.

The Ems also gives access to the Dutch port of Delfzijl and
across the shallow inlet of the Dollart to the narrow and shallow
channel leading to the small Dutch harbour of Nieuw-Statenzijl;
both of these harbours leading in to the Dutch inland waterways
are mentioned in my book *Through The Dutch and Belgian Canals*
(Nautical Books). Entering the Ems you can join Cruise Route 6
Emden to Datteln or Cruise Route 18, the Ems-Jade Canal to
Wilhelmshaven. The Cruise Routes are set out in the second half of
this book.

It is hardly necessary for me to say, I hope, that you will not
consider cruising along this coast without the appropriate charts
and pilot, the *North Sea Pilot, Volume IV*, (55).

The next inlet is the Jade leading in to the Jade-Busen, an area
of drying sands and mud banks or watts, and with the port of
Wilhelmshaven just in to starboard and connecting with Cruise

. . . entrance to the Elbe.

Route 18 already mentioned.

From the Jade the next entry is the Weser, less than 15 kms across from Wilhelmshaven but 70 kms out and around Der Hohe Weg and beyond Alte Mellum on the long legs of the triangle of the buoyed channel. The River Weser leads into Route 1, Bremerhaven to Celle and Route 1A, Bremerhaven to Cuxhaven.

Between the estuaries the dunes continue but picking up the Elbe channel well out on the Elbe 1 Lightship it is from here about 35 kms to Cuxhaven and about 125 kms to Hamburg. Entering the Elbe you lead into Route 2, the Kiel Canal and Route 3, Cuxhaven to Lauenberg.

But many cruising yachtsmen wish to limit the open sea passage and if you have time you can organise your cruise of the German waterways to start from any of the French or Dutch waterway 'front doors' nearest to your home port. Belgium also offers waterway connections with Germany although not direct.

It is surprising, as I have mentioned before, how many
yachtsmen think of the Frisian Islands, Terschelling, Borkum as
being 'up there' and are astonished to learn that the Elbe is on
about the same latitude as the Humber.

The Hook of Holland is on about the same latitude as Harwich
and a little more in distance than a cruise from Southampton to
Le Havre. Next best, in terms of getting into Germany quickly,
to entering a German port is to go in at the Hook and to cruise
through Rotterdam along the Nieuwe Waterweg, the Lek and the
Neder-Rijn, or the Waal, into Germany at Lobith-Emmerich on
Route 11 up the Rhine. You could go in at the Ijsselmeer or
Den Helder or the Nordzee Kanal via Amsterdam or Flushing,
(Vlissingen), from the Westerschelde but the most convenient
entry to Germany through Holland would be at the Hook of
Holland. These Dutch waterways are described in my book
Through The Dutch and Belgian Canals, (Nautical Books), and waterway
connections between Holland and Germany are set out in the 'From
Holland Into Germany' section of this book following the Cruise
Routes.

As already mentioned, Belgium has no direct waterway connec-
tion with Germany but of course you can get to any German
waterway from any Belgian waterway without coming out to sea.
If you cruised up the Wester Schelde to Antwerp and along the
Albert Kanal to Maastricht in Holland you would have to go
either down the Maas—within stone throwing distance of
Germany—to the Waal and there turn right for Lobith-Emmerich
and the Rhine already mentioned OR from Maastricht down
into France and across to Strasbourg. The same considerations
apply whatever Belgian port you enter; you can get into the
European waterway system through Gent, Zeebrugge, Ostend or
Nieuwpoort but you will have to detour through France or
Holland to reach Germany. In my book *Through The Dutch and
Belgian Canals*, I provide details. If you put in at any Belgian harbour
you should make enquiries regarding tax in force at the time.

Most cruising yachtsmen en route to the German waterways
prefer to reach them through France, probably because many
yachts set off from the south coast of England and have Dunkirk,
Calais or Le Havre as their most convenient European 'front
door'. Another splendid reason for cruising into Germany through
France is that you can plan to idle your way DOWN the Rhine
instead of struggling UP; indeed without the power to master the
Rhine current in the worst section (you need a good 8 knots and

even then your engine is sometimes slogging—10 knots preferably), you can still enjoy the German waterways by planning to commence your cruise say from Strasbourg. The Marne route out of Paris to Vitry-le-Francois and then the Canal de la Marne au Rhin to Strasbourg is the usual route. If you did not wish to contemplate the fifty locks from Nancy to Strasbourg you could always turn into the beautiful Moselle just before Nancy and drift down past Luxembourg and the German Moselle wine villages to join the Rhine at Koblenz. But you would then have a job to get back up the Rhine to explore the Main and Neckar for the toughest section of the Rhine is between Koblenz and Mainz.

The routes through France are described in my book *Through The French Canals*, (Nautical Books).

The other German waterway links with adjoining countries are not of much interest unfortunately. The Donau (Danube) rises in the Black Forest near to the Rhine and flows to Ulm where it is an O Class waterway. At Kelheim the Donau is a Class IV waterway for about 130 kms in Germany, then it forms the boundary between Germany and Austria before becoming wholly Austrian, from Austria to form the frontier between Czechoslovakia and Hungary before crossing Hungary into Yugoslavia, becoming the

. . . you need a good 8 knots. The Rhine at St. Goar.

Mellumplate light in
the Jade estuary.

boundary between Yugoslavia and Rumania, and then between
Rumania and Bulgaria, to the Black Sea. The point of mentioning
the wanderings of the Danube in a book on German waterways
is that the new canal link between the Main and Danube, the
Main-Donau-Kanal, will open up an inland shipping route from
the North Sea to the Black Sea within five years. A separate chapter
on this waterway appears on page 130.

Other German waterways that pass behind the Iron Curtain
are the Mittelland Kanal and the Elbe, both leading to Berlin.
There is a fair amount of traffic to and fro across the Iron
Curtain frontiers; the skippers from behind the Curtain are as
friendly as any but you see no Iron Curtain cruising yachtsmen.

Alongside a barge in Hannover we asked the skipper's wife
what would happen if we ignored the frontier signs and chugged
into the German Democratic Republic. She replied without
hesitation that we would be fired upon; but surely not at the
British flag exclaimed my beloved foredeckhand in disbelief?
The skipper only laughed and thought it much more likely that
we would be shot at if we were chugging OUT.

To those adventurous or misguided souls who write to ask for my advice regarding the possibility of a cruise behind the Iron Curtain I usually offer my opinion that the formalities would be interminable, the restrictions irksome and, from what we have glimpsed beyond frontiers, the enjoyment nil.

A final route into Germany is from the Baltic at Lübecker Buht, dealt with in Cruise Route 14, and at the Kiel Canal, Cruise Route 2.

The spelling of German place names in this book will not cause confusion I hope. In the Cruise Routes Section I use the German spelling where it is understandable, (RHEIN, MOSEL), because this is the spelling that you will see when cruising; where names are not understandable the English version is shown in brackets, BRAUNSCHWEIG, (BRUNSWICK). In the rest of the book I use the English versions.

3 Suitable Boats and Equipment

The majority of the German waterways are at least Class IV which means that they can accommodate vessels of 80 m L.O.A., 9 m 50 beam, 2 m 50 draft and 4 m 40 height above the waterline. A draft of 2 m 50 never seems to sound as much as the 8ft it is, but there are not many yachts built today that exceed it. You could take any production cruiser from the London or German Boat Shows and cruise on Class IV waterways without any worry so far as draft is concerned.

At around about 25 m L.O.A. you start exceeding 2 m 50 draft on a motor cruiser and you see few, if any, cruising yachtsmen in the European waterways in craft of this size. At around 17 m L.O.A. you start exceeding 2 m 50 draft in a sailing craft but a sailing yacht is not the most suitable vessel in which to explore the German waterways. The mast-on-deck compromise is all very well in France where you may be enjoying the quieter waterways whilst on your way to the Mediterranean, carrying your mast with you because you propose leaving from a different exit port to your entry port; and in France, of course, you have a great selection of alternative and quiet waterways. In your German cruise you are almost bound to use the Rhine at some time and this river is no place to be in a compromise craft.

Although Class IV waterway dimensions take you over most of the German waterways you would obviously have to consider the limitations of the waterway routes on which you planned to reach Germany. In France, for instance, the Canal de la Marne au Rhin mentioned elsewhere is Class 1, (L.O.A. 38 m 50, beam 5 m, draft 2 m 20 and height above the waterline 3 m 55).

Unfortunately the sort of craft best suited to sail to the German entry ports in the North Sea are least suited for cruising the German inland waterways and vice versa.

Class IV waterway. This is the Dortmund–Ems Canal.

On one occasion, in an eminently suitable-for-the-German-inland-waterways twin-screw motor cruiser we went just from Wilhelmshaven to Bremerhaven. There being no inland route it was necessary to go 'out round' as I mention elsewhere.

In no time at all it seemed after leaving Wilhelmshaven, and running out of the Jade on the ebb, we could look across and watch our destination vanishing astern as we went on out to follow round in the unfriendly navigable channel before we could turn back to Bremerhaven. By the time we had the Mellumplate lighthouse abeam our cruiser was protesting vigorously, writhing and heaving in steep waves and foam, every long heave terminating in a crash that sounded like a supermarket being dropped from a height. We had, we thought, secured everything before leaving. Hanging on to the wheel I could see down through the gap to the saloon below. I watched first the bow climbing and corkscrewing up on to the grey wave and then down from the height into a sickening drop and roll; and then I looked through the gap at the other wave of eggs, coffee, sugar, packets, liquids, flour surging across the saloon carpet, cascading on to the bunks. All we could do was to hang on.

The moral of this sad story is that in the German waters you need horses for courses and this particular motor cruiser was perfect once we were in the inland waterways.

There may be long stretches without locks, such as the Kiel Canal.

Some motor cruisers roll more than others of course.
Displacement hulls roll more than planing hulls, all motor craft
roll more than all sailing craft under sail on most points of the
wind. Part of the answer to the roll of a motor-cruiser is to have
a steadying sail, and another part of the answer is not to go out
in rough weather if you can avoid it.

Every displacement motor-cruiser has a characteristic motion
all its own at sea, some good, some bad. It is necessary to have a
trial run at sea to find out how the craft you fancy behaves.
Another reason for having a trial run is to determine the amount
of engine noise. You must have a diesel engine because petrol is
much more expensive than diesel, even more so abroad; but not
all diesel engines are quiet, even when boat and engine are new.

For a comfortable cruise of the German waterways you need a
good, solid motor cruiser with a speed of at least ten knots. You
should buy as much space as you can afford within a size of hull
that you can manage; for a husband and wife crew this limit
would be about 14m L.O.A. About the only dimension that you
need to consider with care is the height above the waterline.
Modern cruisers seem to be following the American trend of
flying bridges and flying bridges above flying bridges, builders
vying with each other to achieve the greatest altitude.

I have no opinion on the merits of these superstructures
although I do have a friend who sprained his ankle rushing
down from the upper storey to help his wife in a coming
alongside crisis. Motor cruisers with such fixed flying bridges are

useless for the inland waterways but some of the flying bridges are detachable like the wheelhouses of barges. You notice that the big inland waterway ships are generous with all dimensions except height.

Outside Steering Position

An outside steering position is a pleasant feature. An advantage of inland waterway cruising is that there is always something to see and an outside steering position is a grandstand from which you can watch the world go by, particularly in Germany with castles sited spectacularly above you, vineyards climbing steeply up into the sky and but by no means least, the river and lock signals, quite apart from a better awareness, a feel of the throbbing river traffic around you.

Dinghy Stowage

You need a boat that will allow stowage of a dinghy inboard. Dinghies in stern davits can be quite an anxiety when manoeuvring into the small spaces often left for pleasure craft in locks. To tow a dinghy behind you in German waterways would be most unwise. In fact you need everything inboard for peace of mind, including drive units, outside units in my opinion being liable to become lodged on the sills of descending locks.

Catamarans

Catamarans are not suitable for cruising the German waterways by reason of their beam. Sometimes, as mentioned above, the amount of space left for you in locks is quite small, often too small for barges that may have been waiting longer than you and so you are permitted to jump the queue and you

Barges have detachable wheelhouses.

feel quite happy about doing so because you are not taking the place of a working boat. Catamarans and trimarans might well have an anxious time competing for space with the bustling barges of Germany.

Warps

Regarding the equipment you will need for your cruise through the German waterways, warps will be a priority item and the average size cruiser should regard as a minimum four 15 fathom $1\frac{1}{2}$ to 2in. Short lengths of rope, one with a hook spliced on is useful for 'ladder grabbing' in locks and another with an eye splice is handy for dropping over the inset bollards spaced in lock walls as you rise or fall.

Flags

The flags you will need will depend upon your route to Germany and obviously you will have courtesy flags of the countries you pass through. There will be times, probably, when you will need two at the same time, on the Moselle below Trier, for instance, the Luxembourg and German flags on the appropriate sides of the boat. You may be glad of an international code flag 'G' if you need a pilot. You see a number of flags and signals in German waterways and you should obtain the free descriptive booklet of these before setting off. German thoroughness and attention to detail are apparent; motor boats over 10 m LOA have a flag to fly at the bow; a white flag with a horizontal red stripe, the flag to be at least 60 × 60cm. But few are seen although many barges fly a different pattern of red and white.

Fenders and motor tyres are both essential; the fenders for meeting yachts and yachthavens and the tyres for alongside barges and in locks. Four large, sausage shaped fenders are the minimum but do not use them by industrial quays or they become ingrained with oil and grime and they squeeze roll this grime into your topsides.

Motor tyres are most suitable to come between you and your commercial contacts; the small Mini type are most easily handled and stowed. Any garage will be pleased to get rid of as many as you need. They do rather get in the way on deck so that you will probably be able to compromise by having one for each 2 m of waterline.

You do not always want to have motor-tyres hanging over the side as you do in France for there are long stretches without locks in Germany; take with you a supply of flour sacks to cover the tyres which will protect your decks and sides to some extent.

Planks

You will need planks, as long as you can conveniently stow on deck. They will serve two purposes, first to hang outside of the

Two courtesy flags needed: on the left is Luxembourg and on the right is Germany.

tyres when alongside pontoons or piles that would otherwise work their way inside of the tyres and make annoying contact with the hull, second to act as a gangplank for the times when the gap between your boat and the bank is too wide to jump.

Ladders
If you take a ladder as well you can put this out to the shore first and lay the plank along it, giving you extra strength and rigidity. You will appreciate having the ladder onboard when you come alongside an otherwise unscaleable wall.

The stowage on deck of planks and ladder should not hinder a quick and practised drill for the letting go of the anchor. In the German waterways when you need an anchor you need it in a hurry. It sounds facetious to suggest that you make certain the anchor chain is secured inboard but it is a most necessary precaution.

Stakes
There are many places to stop in the German waterways but with nowhere to secure. If you take with you iron stakes, the sort you see at roadworks, with a heavy mallet to knock them in to the river or canal bank, your choice of stopping places will be multiplied a hundredfold.

Boathooks
You need as big a boathook as you can handle, better still two and some long poles if you can find them. Apart from the obvious boathook uses you will need to rig them or the poles to hold you away from banks when you tie up in just sufficient water.

Hooters
A hooter or siren is essential to announce your approach. We use a compressed air siren with a renewable container.

Lights
You will need several torches for the times when you return

to your boat, perhaps along unlighted banks. You must have a riding light to rig at night if you secure in a waterway where traffic moves during the hours of darkness.

Containers

Portable containers in which to carry fuel and water are necessary. Although both are widely available, the time when you run out is sure to be the time when you are miles away from the nearest supply. Filling funnels for each will almost certainly be necessary. Hose we never bother to carry because it takes up so much room and is rarely of the right fitting or length. When a hose would be of value at a supply point it is usually there.

Gas

So much for deck equipment. Below, the first item to consider is the gas supply for cooking and the refrigerator if you have one that runs on gas. You will need a continental adaptor to take Camping Gaz type bottles that are widely available in Germany, also the large butane commercial size cylinders.

If you have a pressurised water system you should take with you a spare pump and the knowledge to fit it.

Busy waterways, such as the scene in Bremen, demand good equipment and a reliable boat.

Carriers   Finally, one useful item that you see coming onboard German yachts is a bottle carrier, the sort that milkmen use with compartments for six or twelve bottles. On Friday nights particularly in German yachting centres you see and hear these containers clanking on deck but I would not swear to it that they all contain milk, in fact I must admit that I have never been offered milk on a German yacht.

However, car-less cruising yachtsmen soon learn to appreciate any load carrying facility.

4 Locks

The locks in German waterways are mostly large and remotely controlled, handling the constant traffic that moves in and out with nonchalant efficiency. First time cruising yachtsmen are understandably a little apprehensive, clutching wheel or tiller as they desperately manoeuvre their ten tons of hull in alongside a thousand-ton barge that a dear old lady has just steered to within an inch of the lock wall whilst peeling the potatoes, doing the washing and attending with expert touch to children, grandchildren, dogs and the big Sulzer diesel; or so it seems. The main thing is that you quickly learn by example and no one stays apprehensive for long.

You obviously possess a certain competence in handling your boat or you would not have got so far as to be approaching a German lock. All that lock work entails is accurately manoeuvring your craft to a predetermined position. If you can place your boat where you want it there is no other aspect of lock procedure to worry about.

I have remarked before that in the big locks you will stay out of trouble if you avoid dithering; in other words move smartly once you have made up your mind to go. Some yachtsmen approach lock shutters as though expecting to be guillotined by them but you can be sure that you will not be if the lights are in your favour.

The medium and large power-operated locks are light controlled, the lights indicating not only Stop and Go but which of several lock approaches you are to enter. In the illustration the barge *Hohentwiel* is moving ahead, the light having changed to green and also indicated which chamber of the locks to enter, the locks in this case being just outside Heidelberg.

As the green light beckons the barge Hohentwiel moves ahead into a lock near Heidelberg.

On smaller waterways the locks are operated by muscle power and you are expected to give a hand. On approaching a small lock, if the gates are closed against you and no one is in view, three toots on your siren will usually produce someone to start opening one gate for you. Whether anyone appears or not, nose your craft into the bank and put a crew member ashore to find the lock keeper if necessary and to open the other gate. If the beam of your boat allows of your entering through one opened

Double lock on the Neckar.

gate, your crew member will go up the lock ladder once inside. Obviously the gates will not be opened for you until the water in the lock chamber is equalised to your level.

If, on approaching, the lock gates are open look to see whether the iron rung ladder is set in the right or left wall. Nose your craft up to the ladder so that your crew can step off on to it carrying a suitable length of attached (to the boat) bow warp coiled over his shoulder like a mountain climber. The crew should get into the habit of gaining the quay quickly and allowing for the pull on the warp once the boat starts moving into the lock. Move on into the lock, the crew will take a turn round a bollard and throw the end of the warp back down to you. If your crew is already ashore to open the gate you will need to have your warp ready coiled to throw and to stand by for its return. Secure aft and be ready to take up as the water rises.

The lock keeper will close one gate behind you and if the second gate has been opened your crew will close that. They will then walk up to the gates ahead and wind up the sluice handles to let the water in. When the lock water level is equalised the lock keeper and your crew will wind open the forward gates, you toss your warp from the bollard, your crew steps on board and you wave goodbye to the lock keeper. This is the procedure for ascending locks.

Descending is easier in that you enter the lock at quay level and can reach out to loop your warp over a bollard. But if, on approach, the gates are closed against you it will still be appreciated by the lock keeper if you put your crew ashore to open the second gate should your boat be unable to squeeze in through the space left by the gate opened by the lock keeper.

Having closed the gates behind you your crew and the lock keeper walk ahead to the forward gates to open the sluices. It is now of the utmost importance to ensure that your warp is not secured both ends on board. If they are, the rope will tighten up as you are lowered in the lock, the deck fitting to which it is attached will be pulled out; or the rope will break; or your boat will be left hanging on the lock wall. If this should happen to you (and it happens to the best of us), shout or sound your siren to have the sluices closed; it may then be necessary to let in some water again to take off the strain and get your warp free. In descending locks you need to be far enough forward in the lock, away from the gates you have entered, to avoid your rudder lodging on the shelf or step just inside the lock.

On the Main-Donau Canal.

Light set at green . . . on the Main.

When you are down to the lower water level your warp is
pulled back onboard; for this reason the warp is passed round the
bollard and not tied to it. You are now low down and your crew
is high up ashore; he rejoins you down the lock ladder or steps at
the foot of which you wait.

Although your crew are free of handle winding chores in the
large power operated locks it is still necessary to put someone
ashore to secure your lines. Since these larger locks are on busier
waterways it is likely that barges will be waiting when you
arrive; they enter according to their place in the queue, only
queue jumping to fill a space that anyone ahead is too big to fill,
usually the fortunate position of the cruising yacht. Even though
you may be the first to arrive at a large lock never assume that
you should be the first to enter. Lock keepers prefer to get the
large and awkward barges in first and then filling the remaining
space as best they can.

When your turn arrives you must be ready to move forward
promptly, with a member of your crew on the foredeck holding a
suitable warp at the ready as you steer for a lock ladder. If it is
more convenient to come alongside a barge do so. There is not
likely to be any objection unless he is displaying a 'No one
onboard' sign which petrol barges sometimes do alongside their
'No smoking' sign. If you secure to a barge it saves you all the

"No one on board" sign beside
"No smoking" sign.

bother with your own warps but be ready to cast off from him
before he or any other barge is ready to leave. Barges leaving
locks sometimes create considerable turbulence in the water as
their screws thrash to get under way and you must be secured to
the lock wall at this time.

With the lock closed and the lights against you it will be
necessary to secure alongside in the lock approaches out of the
way of commercial traffic. Try not to take a place that a bigger
craft could more conveniently use. Some convoys need a lot of
room when they stop and you do not want to be in the middle of
it. You should never secure for the night in the approach to a
lock. If you drift in the stream waiting for the water in the lock
to equalise to your level you must watch for the influence of the
current to or from the lock.

A number of locks and lock approaches have closed-circuit
television. The lock controller ahead may be able to watch your
movements and you are not aware of his existence until a voice
seemingly from the clouds identifies your craft by name.

Many locks are free and times of opening vary. The Moselle
locks, for instance, are open round the clock and make no charge
for a yacht locking through with a commercial craft. Only if they
have to do any work solely on your account do you have to pay
for it.

It will be obvious that locks operated from, and into, tidal
waterways are regulated according to the tides.

Where locks are so deep that they would need all your warps
together to reach from the bottom of the chamber to the lock
quay and back there is no need to start vigorously joining them
with sheet bends. Inset bollards are recessed down the sides of
deep lock walls and you transfer your warp from one to another
as you rise or fall. No crew is put ashore. If you are placed near
to a ladder rather than the recessed bollards you use your
ladder-hooking method. If the lock is wide enough and the
arrangement of barges in the lock permits, you secure to a barge.

Through the German Waterways

The following illustrations show the sequence of movement in a deep lock at Minden:

In . . .

. . . up

. . . out . . . from Minden lock.

Lock gates take many forms. Most are hinged and swing as their name implies, some recede into the lock wall. They are pleasant vantage points on which to lean ones elbows and ruminate; crew often stand here, even on the gates of remote control locks, drawn by force of winding habit and association of that spot with pleasant chats with lock keepers. The lock gate at Minden is one on which the crew would be ill advised to ruminate.

. . . no place to ruminate.

The Minden lock raises or lowers craft 13m in a few minutes without a ripple, an operation that involves 12,000cbm of water but the canal is not emptied of this amount at each operation. Both sides of the lock chamber have four compartments which take up, one after the other, the greatest part of the water on the downwards lock from out of the lock chamber and only about a third of the water empties into the River Weser. On the upward lock the reservoir chamber compartments empty themselves one after the other back into the lock chamber.

5 Planning the Cruise . . . . . .
In the Waterways of Germany

No formalities are required to take your boat into Germany provided that it is under 15 tons displacement as explained later. There is no need to seek planning permission as was once necessary in France. If you plan a cruise to Germany through France you will probably have heard that the French no longer require the issue of a *Permis de Circulation* and that the Green Card, (*Passeport du navire étranger*), is not now obtainable in advance but issued by French Customs at your French port of entry.

If you happen to be a member of a yacht club you could carry your membership card but the principal frontier documents required for Germany are valid passports for each person onboard. The Certificate of Registry and the Ship Insurance should also be with you.

But first of all you will want to plan your cruise of Germany and when you have decided upon the areas you would like to visit the Cruise Routes and the Cruise Route Map will show you which routes are appropriate.

Since the most attractive parts of Germany tend to be at the 'bottom end' and the industrial parts at the 'top end' you should seriously consider the suggestion to come into Germany from France, say at Strasbourg.

You could then glide down the Rhine on Cruise Route 8 to Mannheim for a cruise of the River Neckar on Cruise Route 13; from your mooring at Heidelberg you would see the castle floodlit and firework displays if you were there on a first Saturday in July, August or September.

Back at Mannheim to rejoin Cruise Route 8 to Mainz and you could explore the Main on Cruise Route 12, a voyage through

'The Rhine in flames'.

wooded settings and villages of wine and half-timbered houses.

Returning to Mainz and the Rhine on Cruise Route 8 you would race down through the gorge of castles and wine. On the third Saturday in September the castles are floodlit, a wonderful spectacle conveniently seen from St. Goar.

Cruise Route 8 runs on to Koblenz where you should contrive to be on the second Saturday in August to see 'The Rhine in Flames'. The beautiful valley of the Lahn is nearby on Cruise Route 7.

At Cologne on Cruise Route 11 there is a boat procession earlier in the year at Corpus Christi.

And away over and through the smoke, along the Mittelland Kanal and down the Weser on Cruise Route 16 you can dance behind the Pied Piper of Hamelin on every summer Sunday and watch the children dressed as rats performing the Rat Dance.

And still you have the magic Moselle to fit in somewhere, perhaps to conclude your German cruise on Cruise Route 9, another voyage of romantic castles and wine villages. On what better note could your cruise of Germany end than a tour of Moselle wine festivals early in September, leaving you with memories of Bernkasteler Doktor and Moselle smoked eel?

Before you recovered from such a delicious experience you might have drifted down the Saône and Rhône to winter in the Mediterreanean. I am not referring to the sort of cruise that you could undertake in a holiday of two weeks as you will probably guess.

In the Cruise Routes Section some stopping places are given but the number of stopping places is obviously almost limitless. I can cruise through a country and stop at a thousand places and you can cruise through and stop at a thousand more. Comparing notes with other boats we are no longer surprised to find how rarely we can call 'Snap' to identical stopping places we have found; obviously in many towns you go to the same harbours but there are some miles of bank and quayside outside of the big harbours in Germany.

Frequently you pass places where you stopped last time, or was it the time before? Frequently you aim for that pleasant place that was so comfortable the last time but are overtaken by the approach of darkness—no time schedule of any two trips ever seems to match up—or perhaps there is now a grain discharger there. Sometimes you stop in good time at a fairly indifferent place but you stop there because you recognise it and next morning pass a dreamy looking spot only five minutes further on

The Rhine at Bad Godesberg. Line up the mast of the struggling upcoming barge on the castle to compare progress from top picture to bottom—in the time that the downstream barge is borne swiftly out of the picture.

that you promised to explore next time. But of course, even if you could get the timing right always to stop at places you know you would then be failing to discover new places; and bankside discoveries of your own always possess a special charm which is not to say that one does not appreciate Germany's claim to have over three hundred INLAND harbours.

The most important rule is to fix an absolute deadline for stopping, a deadline that allows ample time to explore in daylight. It is very tempting to see what lies around just one more bend but you must resist the temptation.

If you start looking early enough you will always find somewhere; even in the heavy traffic waterways it is often possible to find a backwater out of the disturbance of the main stream. Do not be afraid to explore. You will be surprised to find what a splendid ambassador your flag is almost everywhere in Germany.

You may want maps of the various waterways as a matter of interest but you will not need them from a navigational point of view. The most difficult waterway sections to negotiate are on the Rhine but they are comparatively short sections in relation to the length of the river. You can buy a Rheinatlas and popular type strip maps quite cheaply. The Rhine is so busy that there is always a vessel to follow.

You are supposed to have onboard the *Rheinschiffartpolizeiverordnung* for the Rhine, the *Moselschiffahrtpolizeiverordnung* for the Moselle and the *Binnenschiffartstrassenordnung* for all other waterways except the Donau that you cannot reach at the moment. It may seem odd to have onboard rules that you may not understand, (it is the same in Holland with the *Rijnvaartpolitiereglement*), but a copy of the *Rheinschiffartpolizeiverordnung* prominently displayed in the wheelhouse creates the right impression upon visiting the Rhine Shipping Police of whom more later.

You can obtain these publications from most booksellers in Germany or from the Inland Shipping publishers at 41 Duisburg, 13 Haus Rhein, Dammstrasse 15–17. I have received excellent service from *Rheinschiffart*, 68 Mannheim 1, Haus Oberrhein.

The Germans are incredibly thorough in everything they do and when it comes to conduct on their inland waterways you can imagine that they practically organise a rule of the road for the fish. (There is a rule prohibiting mooring by, or in, reeds where fish are breeding).

The Rhine is a tough river carrying a lot of traffic and you can understand the need for some sort of driver's licence or evidence

Commercial hordes on the Rhine.

of ability before anyone is allowed to do battle with the commercial hordes on this river; indeed this is the case with German nationals for any sizeable craft. Some years ago a lady we know in Cologne told us that she had qualified for her Captain's Certificate as she called it which caused us to wonder if she had joined the Merchant Marine at an advanced age but, in fact, it was a permit authorising her to take the wheel of her own large cruiser on the Rhine.

The traffic regulations for travel on the German Federal Waterways are as follows, (three have already been mentioned):

Seeschiffahrtstrassenordnung
or Sea Shipping Regulations.
These apply to coastal areas and the tidal Ems, Weser, Hunte, Oste, Elbe, Eider, Trave and the Nord-Ostsee Kanal.
Rheinschiffahrtpolizeiverordnung
or Rhine Shipping Police Rules which apply to the Rhine.

Moselschiffahrtpolizeiverordnung
or Moselle Shipping Police Rules which apply to the Moselle.
Donauschiffahrtpolizeiverordnung
or Danube Shipping Police Rules
which apply to the Danube and will be of interest to us once the
Danube can be reached through the Main-Donau Kanal.
Binnenschiffahrtstrassenordnung
or Inland Shipping Police Rules which apply to all other
waterways.

Besides these traffic regulations there are additional Shipping
Police Orders which have been made by the Waterways and
Shipping Directorate.

Included in these rules is a lot of basic seamanship and navigation that you will know and will not want repeated. You will
want reproduced explanations of signs that you are likely to meet
and these are given.

For yachts of under 15 tons displacement there is no need at the
moment to obtain a Pilot's Certificate to cruise in the Federal
Waterways. But, says the *Bundesminister für Verkher*, (Transport),
one must expect that the piloting of motor boats will require a
pilot's certificate in the near future.

For piloting a yacht, (the term used is sports boat), of more
than 15 tons displacement you need:
on the Rhine
a Rheinschifferpatent or driving licence
on other waterways, (except the Danube that does not concern us)
simply a certificate to say that you are capable.

As in most countries there is a minimum age limit of 16 which
in Germany applies to all craft under 15 tons displacement on all
waterways; for craft over 15 tons displacement the minimum age
is 21 on the Rhine and 23 on other waterways.

The certificate of competence mentioned above is little more
than a formality so far as foreign yachtsmen are concerned
because it is reasonably assumed that if you have managed to
get to Germany you must possess the necessary ability. The matter
of the *Rheinschifferpatent* is not so easily disposed of. As you can
imagine, if you are asked for your non-existent 'Patent' a lengthy
debate regarding the tonnage of your craft ensues and the police
are very friendly. We have not been in difficulties on this account
because we have calculated our displacement under the limit
but it seems that the Rhine police may enquire at places in front
of difficult Rhine sections where there are pilots of course.

Obviously you can proceed with a pilot onboard because he possesses a *Rheinschifferpatent* and you may well be glad of him through the hazard.

If you wanted to engage a pilot you could do so from the Labour Office Duisburg, 41 Duisburg 13, Schifferbörse or from the General Employers' Union for Rhine Shipping at 41 Duisburg 13, Haus Rhein.

There are no special rules concerning your boat provided that it is under 15 tons displacement and provided that it is properly 'marked' for identification purposes, (plus the name and address of the owner clearly marked inside).

Craft of over 15 tons displacement need a Certificate of Seaworthiness to travel on the Federal Waterways BUT since you will have crossed the sea to be in the inland waterways of Germany for which your seaworthiness must be proved, this is recognised to the extent that you need only produce a Certificate of Travelworthiness. This certificate can be issued by your club or 'any office for such purpose', so there should be little difficulty so long as you get it before leaving home.

If you are in the over 15 tons displacement category it is worthwhile going to the trouble of obtaining a nice looking piece of paper on these lines even though it is not very likely that you will need it.

In Germany a Certificate of Seaworthiness is issued after inspection of the vessel by the Shipping Inspection Commission who have offices at Emden, Münster, Duisburg, Köln, Koblenz, Mainz, Mannheim, Heilbronn, Würzburg, Regensburg, Minden, Kiel, Bremen, Hamburg, Berlin and Lübeck so that you can see there is not much chance of selling your old 'tore out' to a German.

In exceptional cases the Shipping Inspection Commission can give to a vessel without a valid certificate a special Permit for one single journey which then takes the place of the Shipping Certificate.

At the conclusion of so much comment on the subject of displacement you may be wondering if your craft is over or under the qualifying 15 tons displacement mentioned. It is a surprisingly elusive figure whereas comparatively useless formula dimensions like Thames tonnage and net tonnage are freely available, the latter particularly so on the main beam of your craft if registered.

A rough and ready formula for ascertaining the displacement

tonnage of a motor-cruiser type hull is:
WL length × WL breadth × average draft × .45
= cubic capacity in feet.
Divided by 35 this gives displacement tonnage.

I am aware that many yachtsman have cruised in Germany
for years without the slightest fuss about the tonnage of their
craft and will probably continue to do so, but the rules outlined
are stated by the responsible authority to be the rules today.

On arrival in Germany you hardly have time to bother with a
Customs flag before you are alongside efficient Customs points
but you will, of course, have your German courtesy flag hoisted
on your starboard side.

Navigational directions, signals and lights are well illustrated in
Sicherheit auf dem Wasser that can be obtained free by writing to
ADAC AM Westpark 8, 8000, Munchen 70.

At first the barge and shipping traffic will appear to be
scattered all over your line of approach but you soon get
accustomed to the receding pattern of it. You have to get
accustomed to the volume and power of the shipping traffic and
to the power of the big river too if you have not come in that
way. On most rivers you can move through the water feeling
your command, you can turn wheel or tiller this way and that
and get the instant response of your boat in charge of the water;
but the Rhine is a real strong character. Give a little too much
helm and your whole front end is swept away on the current
and you quickly realise that you are dealing with a giant.

The power of this giant is felt most dramatically in the Rhine
Gorge on Cruise Route 8. There are signal stations through the
bends of the gorge to warn shipping struggling up of shipping
swooping down for the up-coming traffic can at least stop. In this
short stretch of 25kms or so is packed one of the most dramatic
nautical experiences of any waterway in Europe, but at least you
are never alone. The constant stream of traffic there ensures that
you have a guide.

The rule of the road is, of course, to keep to the right. The
exception to this rule is the deep laden barge that is obliged to
follow the deep water channel whichever side of the waterway
this takes her. Prior to coming over to your side she will put out
from the starboard side of the wheelhouse a large blue flag and
you should then alter course to pass her on the blue flag side.
This you would certainly do on the narrower waterways but the
big rivers in Germany are so wide that you hold your course and
stay where you are. The deep laden vessel needs so much depth

There are signal stations through the bends of the gorge, such as near Loreley.

that there will be plenty for you between her and your river bank.

Blue flags are quite often acknowledged by approaching vessels who signal understanding of the blue flag change of course although on the Rhine at times every barge in sight seems to be blue flagging. You may hear sound signal acknowledgement being given. The cruising yachtsmen on the bigger rivers is looked upon as fry too small to play this game and nothing more than keeping out of the way is expected of him although the cruising yacht is not absolved from making definite sound signals when emerging from waterway side turnings.

A blue flag displayed right forward is an overtaking sign, not, you would think, worth bothering with but some loaded vessels take a long time to get past long tows.

At night flashing lights are used instead of blue flags but I sincerely hope that you will not contemplate cruising on the German waterways after the hours of darkness. For this reason I have not thought it necessary to include night signals.

You must make sure of being snugged up in as quiet a berth
as you can find well before dark. Once darkness descends shipping
appears to assume twice the volume, twice the size and twice
the speed of day, while navigation lights, bridge lights, and shore
lights join forces to confuse you. Vast hulls as big as a warehouse
glide past you at frightening speed, nonchalant men up in the
dimly lighted wheelhouses of pushers urge their linked barge
loads, as big as a football pitch it seems, thrusting ahead into the
black night.

While it is perfectly safe to hold your course and keep going
when meeting 'blue flag' vessels you must make a distinction over
passenger steamers that may be coming in to the bank to land or
take on passengers. No problem of understanding arises; if a
passenger ship is slowing down it is likely to be going into a
landing stage so you will see this and act accordingly.

Ferries are a different matter, crossing continually from bank to
bank, so you must judge the best moment to pass them. The
large, vehicle-carrying ferries, independently manoeuvring under

Passenger steamers, Cologne.

their own power, will stop for ships but will not want to stop for you. With the smaller ferries it is simply a matter of judgement and consideration.

Meeting barges on the few narrow canals you must slow down as you wait for the approach and ease in towards the bank on your side as far as you dare. As the bow wave approaches you increase your speed and again when you are amidships of her, aiming back into the centre of the channel through the wash of her screw.

It is likely that you will be the overtaken vessel most of the time on the wide waterways and you will be overtaken without comment just as you will overtake the odd slower craft that you come up to. If you keep well over to your side of the channel you will not attract attention but if you are in the way you will soon hear about it.

The busiest waterways are the Rhine to Duisburg-Ruhrort and then up to Koblenz, the Elbe to Hamburg and the Kiel Canal. Then that part of the Rhine to Mainz, the Weser to Bremen, also Wilhelmshaven; next the Rhine to the frontier, the Ems to Emden, the Mittelland Kanal, the Dortmund-Ems Kanal, Moselle and then the Neckar and Main.

The upper speed limit on the Rhine is 12km per hour but on this and other waterways speed limits vary and are indicated by a restriction sign. There will always be other traffic to serve as a guide but the following limits have been noted:–

	Kms per hour
Aller	12
Datteln-Hamm Kanal	10
Dortmund-Ems Kanal	9
Elbe-Lübeck Kanal	8
Elisabethfehn Kanal	6
Ems	6
Ilmenau	7
Küsten Kanal	9
Lahn	10
Leda	6
Mittelland Kanal	10
Neckar	14
Rhine-Herne Kanal	12
Wesel-Datteln Kanal	11

Speed limits are imposed not only out of consideration for other waterway users but to safeguard the banks and shore activities from wash. On the big rivers the speed and size of passing craft raises such a wash that you cannot have anything of value free-standing. You can imagine what effect this wash is having as it rolls up the shore and you will see appropriate 'Wash' signs here and there.

The bother of being rocked by the wash of passing big ships is as nothing to the hazard of being sucked in towards them as they pass. Even if there was no rule obliging you to keep out of the way you would soon learn to keep well out of the way of the big fast moving vessels, to be aware of their gliding up behind you and of the line they will have to take in passing you in relation to approaching craft.

In dodging other craft or crossing the fairway to join another cruise route you should take particular care before deciding to pass behind tugs, sometimes towing barges so far behind them that, at first sight, they appear to have nothing to do with each other. In no time at all you appreciate that flag signals, such as towing signals, really mean what they say.

For the cruising yachtsman in Germany there are no special problems about navigation in relation to the avoidance of commercial shipping, (all of which will be larger than you), because the rules for you can be summed up in five words:
KEEP OUT OF THE WAY.

Mittelland Canal.

6 Cost of Living and Shopping

When we first cruised into Germany after the war the rate of exchange was 11.68 DM's to the £. Only ten years ago it was 11.13. Now you get three if you are lucky. The odd thing is that relative prices do not seem to reflect this worsening of the exchange rate.

The causes behind fluctuations in money values are all quite beyond me and all I can do—in common with every foreign visitor everywhere who calculates and mutters prior to every purchase abroad—is to relate value to the latest equivalent at home. Of course, when you are away for six months or more at a time, as we are, the values at home tend to have sprouted a little from the comparative base that we have been using.

Let us say that we manage in Germany today as well as we manage in any other country mainly because we have to and because you can live cheaply anywhere on a boat if you set your mind to it. Returning holidaymakers who complain of high prices in countries abroad are judging by a completely different set of of standards to those of the cruising yachtsman. For instance before we set off on this most recent trip we had a sophisticated and knowledgeable gentleman onboard who spent most of his time in Germany and who warned us of the prohibitive cost of everything there quoting, as an example, the price he had been required to pay for a flat in Frankfurt. When questioned he did not know the price of meat or vegetables because, being unmarried, he always ate in restaurants; he did not even know the price of a Frankfurter. When we compared in detail it turned out that his living expenses for a week would have kept us very nicely on our boat in Germany for a month or more.

This is the point that I never tire of explaining to would-be cruising yachtsmen and their wives. Once you have your boat the cruising life is the most economical travelling life you could wish for. Even the hitchhiker has to eat at shore prices whilst you are cooking your own. A cruising yachtsman, (though not necessarily his wife to the same extent), has a lot of the instincts of a hobo and you find that you live happily on very little.

In France we experiment with wine. Whatever country we are in we always seem to be experimenting; whatever country we are in we always seem to have a friendly boat alongside whose crew return from shopping over our decks or we return over theirs. Shopping comparisons in these circumstances are never odious. With drink, comparisons are an excuse for drinking; not, of course, to quench ones thirst but for the delectation of one's palate and one's soul; and where else in the world does a bottle look so fine as upon a cabin table, with friends snugged in around, resting and glowing under the dancing shadows of the Tilley lamp.

In Germany it is the Rhine wine and the Moselle wine, the schnaps and the beer. German red wines, as you probably know, are not in the same league as the white. And when the wine has flowed a little our comparisons turn to . . . sausages.

A sausage in Germany is known as a *Wurst*. Ready to eat sausages, (no cooking required), are the *METTwurst*, *KATEN-wurst*, *SCHINKENwurst* and *BIERwurst*; like pâté, for spreading on toast, are the *LEBERwurst* and *TEEwurst*; for warming the *BOCKwurst*; for frying the *BRATwurst*; the varieties are endless.

The Wonderful World of the German sausage.

Economical living is helped along a lot in Germany if you can get to like the staple diet of sausage; amongst all the varieties there simply must be one that appeals to your palate. If you start with one that is plain and lightly spiced you can from there explore the wonderful world of the sausage, as varied as the world of wine if somewhat less romantic. The nutrition of the German sausage is unrivalled although you may imagine that you do not care for some of the ingredients.

Also nutritionally excellent is the German dark bread, dark of course because it is made from unrefined flour unlike our own white bread of blotting paper consistency. What more could you ask than to sit in the cockpit by the river bank eating pumpernickel and cheese and drinking dark beer? There are hundreds of varieties of bread in Germany, wheat bread and rye bread, black, brown or white. The dark wholemeal *Vollkornbrot* is supposed to go best with the *wurst* mentioned above.

There are shops everywhere convenient to almost every waterway. At many bakers' shops, or *bäckeri*, you see people having coffee with the tempting pastries. In the milk shops, or *mölkerei*, snacks are also served.

The pavement cafe habit is a pleasant way of passing the time but the beer that the waiter brings you will cost a third of the price in a supermarket. We do not eat ashore very much because we are happier to provide onboard and it always seems such a fuss to turn out of our cosy cabin for an evening meal; although the main meal in Germany has traditionally been the mid-day

Pavement cafe in
Bremen.

meal, (after the early morning breakfast and the mid-morning breakfast). It is easier to be tempted to eat ashore when you are already ashore and the solid *Gasthof* beckons and you know that *Kasseler Rippenspeer* is smoked loin of pork and that *Rheinischer Sauerbraten* is crumbly roast beef in slices as thick as a prayer book with all sorts of cooked fruit as mouth-watering accompaniment. If you prefer fish you find trout available everywhere, *Gedünste Forelle* being poached and *Gebackene Forelle* fried.

Hamburg *Flunder*, flounder with bacon, is more of a coastal speciality as is Bremer *Aalfrikassel* of mixed fish but with eel predominating.

To accompany main courses are potatoes and vegetables, fruit and, of course, sauerkraut which, as you know, is slightly sour shredded cabbage. Sauerkraut has been a staple European dish for hundreds of years and still is.

Before you have recovered you are being offered *Apfelstrudel* with cream or cherry cake, (*Kirschtorte*).

Festival of the national drink,—beer.

Beer is the national drink and Germany is probably near to the top of the world brewing and drinking league. Light beer is *Helles*, strong light beer *Heller Bock*; and dark beer is *Dunkles*, strong dark beer *Dunkler Boch*.

There are many varieties and you could link up your sampling programme with your sausage tasting experiments since they go together. A *Würstlerei*, in fact, is just the place to visit for this purpose for they sell nothing but sausages and beer.

In some drinking establishments in Germany you are offered beer and schnaps together, or as a chaser although I am not sure which chases what. The first time I was introduced to this practice I stepped from the river bank on to a gangplank that was not underneath my foot at all and I have been careful with Schnaps chasers ever since.

Most German wines do not travel well but Germany produces probably the best white wine in the world. With a production only a tenth that of France the place to get to know the German wines is in the wine villages of the Middle Moselle such as Bernkastel, Zeltingen, Klüsserath, Trittenheim and Piesport, to name a few, or the Rheingau at Rüdesheim, Erbach or Eltville, Rheinhessen at Nierstein and Oppenheim, besides Franconian wines on the Main at Würzburg. Where else would you find so many wine villages accessible to the cruising yacht, many with alongside moorings of their own or nearby.

If you are seeking a bargain from the extensive shopping displays in all German towns you need to have already in mind what your proposed bargain would cost at the discount stores in this country. With the German reputation for camera quality, for instance, you would probably put camera equipment high on your list of desirables and would expect to get a bargain in the country of origin. It is not necessarily so, even ignoring Customs duty, because prices are fixed in Germany.

Brief food vocabulary

ENGLISH	GERMAN	ENGLISH	GERMAN
Apple	*Apfel*	Haddock	*Schellfisch*
Apricot	*Aprikose*	Hake	*Seehecht*
Asparagus	*Spargel*	Halibut	*Heilbutt*
Bacon	*Speck*	Ham	*Schinken*
Baker	*Bäcker*	Herring	*Hering*
Banana	*Banane*	Honey	*Honig*
Beef	*Rindfleisch*	Ice	*Eis*
Beefsteak	*Rindflseisch-*	Jam	*Konfitüre*
	schnitte	Kidney Beans	*Französische bohne*
Beer	*Bier*	Kidneys	*Sorte*
Beetroot	*Rote Rübe*	Lamb	*Lamm*
Bread	*Brot*	Lemon	*Zitrone*
Brussels Sprouts	*Rozenkohl*	Lettuce	*Salat*
Butcher	*Metzger, Fleischer*	Liver	*Lebende*
Butter	*Butter*	Lobster	*Hummer*
Cabbage	*Kohl*	Mackerel	*Makrele*
Can Opener	*Büchsenöffner*	Margarine	*Margarine*
Carrot	*Mohrrübe*	Marrow	*Knochenmark*
Cauliflower	*Blemenkohl*	Meat	*Fleisch*
Celery	*Sellerie*	Milk	*Milch*
Cheese	*Käse*	Mushroom	*Pilz*
Chemist	*Chemiker-drogist*	Mussel	*Muschel*
Cherry	*Kirsche*	Mustard	*Senf*
Chicken	*Huhn, Kücken*	Mutton	*Hammelfleisch*
Chop	*Kotelett*	Oil	*Öl*
Cocoa	*Kakao*	Olive	*Olive*
Cod	*Kabeljau*	Onion	*Zwiebel*
Coffee	*Kaffee*	Orange	*Orange*
Confectioners	*Zuckerbäcker*	Oysters	*Auster*
Crab	*Krabbe*	Parsnip	*Pastinake*
Cream	*Rahm*	Peach	*Pfirsich*
Cucumber	*Gurke*	Pear	*Birne*
Cutlet	*Kotelett*	Peas	*Erbse*
Duck	*Ducken*	Pineapple	*Ananas*
Egg	*Ei*	Plaice	*Scholle*
Fig	*Feige*	Plum	*Pflaume*
Fish	*Fisch*	Pork	*Schweinefleisch*
Flour	*Mehl*	Potato	*Kartoffel*
French Beans	*Schnittbohne*	Prawn	*Steingarnele*
Frog '	*Frosch*	Rabbit	*Kaninchen*
Fruit	*Frucht*	Raspberry	*Himbeere*
Grape	*Weintraube*	Rhubarb	*Rhabarber*
Grapefruit	*Pampelmuse*	Salmon	*Lachs*
Grocer	*Kolonialwaren-*	Salt	*Salz*
	händler	Sausage	*Wurst*

ENGLISH	GERMAN	ENGLISH	GERMAN
Slice	*Schnitte*	Thrush	*Drossel*
Snail	*Schnecke*	Tin	*Zinn*
Sole	*Seezunge*	Tomato	*Tomate*
Soup	*Suppe*	Tripe	*Kaldaunen*
Spinach	*Spinat*	Trout	*Forelle*
Strawberry	*Erdbeere*	Turbot	*Steinbutt*
Sugar	*Zucker*	Turnip	*Rübe*
Sweetbread	*Kalbfleisch*	Veal	*Kalbfleisch*
Tart	*Torte*	Vinegar	*Essig*
Tea	*Tee*	Water	*Wasser*

Boat vocabulary

ENGLISH	GERMAN	ENGLISH	GERMAN
Acid	*Sauer*	Fill Up	*Voll machen,*
Armature	*Bewaffnung*		*Auffüllen*
Battery	*Batterie*	Insulating Tape	*Isolierband*
Bolt	*Bolzen*	Oil	*Öl*
Carburettor	*Vergaser*	Petrol	*Benzin*
Diesel	*Diesel*	Screw	*Schraube*
Distributor	*Verteiler*	Screw Driver	*Schraubenzieher*
Dynamo	*Dynamo*	Self Starter	*Selbstanlasser*
Engine	*Motor*	Spanner	*Schraubenschlüssel*

7 Weather and Miscellaneous Items of Interest

WEATHER What is known as the tourist season extends from May to October but we have had a layer of ice in the cockpit in May and glorious sunshine and blossom in April so that the weather pattern is much like our own.

The regular boat services start on the Rhine in mid-April and carry on until late October.

In July and August holiday facilities are crowded as they are everywhere.

In the North Sea area the weather is inclined to be cloudy and damp with a good chance of pleasant weather in the spring. Any seasonal forecast would be as dependable as our own weather. Obviously you would not set out for the German North Sea ports without the most up to date information.

PUBLIC HOLIDAYS 1 January New Year's Day
Easter from Good Friday to Easter Monday
1 May May Day
Ascension Day
Whit Monday
17 June—Day of Unity
20 November—Prayer and Repentance Day
Christmas

MAIL Can be sent to you, Poste Restante, to selected post offices in towns

SHOP HOURS 0800 to 1830 weekdays
0800 to 1400 Saturdays

BANK   0830 to 1300
HOURS   1430 to 1600 (Fridays 1800)
          closed Saturdays

DUTY   At the time of writing there are Duty Free Fuel advantages and
FREE   you should enquire of Customs and Police at your port of entry
FUEL   if the concession is available to you at the time of your visit.

WEIGHTS
AND
MEASURES

litres		gals		kms		miles
1	=	0,22		1	=	0,62
2	=	0,44		2	=	1,24
3	=	0,66		3	=	1,86
4	=	0,88		4	=	2,48
5	=	1,10		5	=	3,11
6	=	1,32		6	=	3,73
7	=	1,54		7	=	4,35
8	=	1,76		8	=	4,97
9	=	1,98		9	=	5,59
10	=	2,20		10	=	6,21
15	=	3,30		15	=	9,32
20	=	4,40		20	=	12,43
30	=	6,60		30	=	18,64
40	=	8,80		40	=	24,85
50	=	11,00		50	=	31,07
100	=	22,00		100	=	62,14

kgs		lbs
0,453	=	1
0,907	=	2
1,360	=	3
1,814	=	4
2,268	=	5
2,721	=	6
3,175	=	7
3,628	=	8
4,082	=	9
4,535	=	10

8 Route Detail Section

WATERWAYS shown in CAPITAL letters refer to the Route that you are following . . .
WATERWAYS shown in *italics* refer to waterways leading off . . .
DIVERSIONS from the main route are shown between broken lines . . .

Molln.

List of Place Names—and Appropriate Cruise Route Numbers

List of Place Names and appropriate Cruise Route Numbers
(continued)

left bank

Alphabetical List of Waterways

Between Bad Essen and Getmold on the Mittelland Canal.

Route 1 **Bremerhaven to Celle**

Distance	203 kms
Number of locks	6
Minimum height above water	4m 50
Minimum depth of water	1m 70

Kms Locks

UNTER-WESER

BREMERHAVEN. Entering the broad Unter-Weser from the North Sea you pass the eight big ship basins, petrol tanks, chimneys, cranes, the Bremerhaven Ocean Terminal, 'Columbus Quay', that can handle five ocean liners simultaneously, and proceed bearing in slightly to port when you will see the light towers at the end of the short moles at the entrance to the River Geeste and the fishing boat harbours. Sounding the required warning you enter between the towers and lock in to the Fischereihaven.

Every second fish eaten in Germany comes from here; you should stir from your bunk to see the early morning fish auctions. The smell of fish is, of course, all pervading.

Bremerhaven is a big container terminal and Germany's leading passenger port. Shipbuilding is a big industry.

There is a fine promenade, seaside zoo, North Sea aquarium. The Morgan-Stern Museum, (shipping history, ship models), is by the Weser Yacht Club.

2   **NORDENHAM**

13   **RODENKIRCHEN**

10   **BRAKE.** A small commercial harbour.

11   **ELSFLETH**
(Connect Route 5)

(from R. River Hunte)

30   **BREMEN.** Coming up the broad river on the tide you are passed by ships big and small and as you

Bremerhaven.

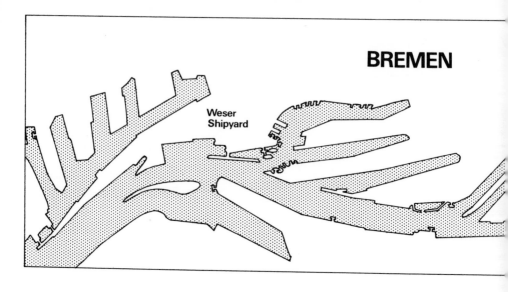

BREMEN

Weser
Shipyard

Km Locks

UNTER-WESER

Bremen (cont.)

Route 1

cruise through this major port and look along each crowded basin you wonder where newly arriving big ships can possibly find a space; so crowded nose to tail are the big ships already berthed that you imagine the new arrivals cruising around like hopeful car parkers enquiring of captains if they are leaving yet. For it is not the occasional ship that passes you but a constant stream: this is the second largest port in Germany with an average of thirty-five ships calling every day. Famous for ship-building, Bremen also supplies vast quantities of beer.

By the A.G. Weser shipyards, (capable of building ships up to 500,000 tons), the river bends and you see the spires and the bridges ahead; after the third bridge, the Weserbrücke, you can secure to port by the Tiefer Osterdeich. It is a very pleasant and convenient place to be. The Market Square is nearby with the Statue of Roland, 1404, Town Hall, 1405, and Town Hall Tavern, the Ratskeller, one of the oldest municipal wine cellars in Germany, dating from 1408 and offering you a choice of five hundred wines. St. Peter's Cathedral 11th Century; several museums and art gallery; Rhododendron Park with over 900 different kinds; Zoo.

1

12   **ACHIM**

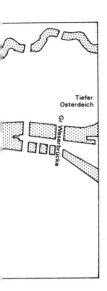

Tiefer
Osterdeich

Gr. Weserbrücke

Kms	*Locks*	Route 1
	I	
LEFT, RIVER ALLER 12		
(R. Mittel-Weser)		
3		**VERDEN.** A market town.
		(Connect Route 16)
31		**RETHEM**

— —

RIGHT,		
RIVER LEINE		
21		**NEUSTADT**
MITTELLAND-		
KANAL 12		

— —

RIVER ALLER		
	4	
79		**CELLE.** An attractive place of timbered houses and
		a famous centre of orchid growing. Town Hall 16thC.

Route 1A **Bremerhaven to Cuxhaven**

A short cut and inland passage to the Elbe from Bremerhaven. Although a map shows Cuxhaven to be 'just round the corner' from Bremerhaven a chart reveals a very different picture, with Wurster Watt and sands extending beyond the island of Neuwerk; in fact the buoyed fairway of the Elbe commences about four miles eastward of Elbe 1 light-vessel.

Distance	66 kms
Number of locks	3
Minimum height above water	2m 90
Minimum depth of water	1m 20

RIVER GEESTE
(tidal to first lock)

BREMERHAVEN
(Connect Route 1)

Bremerhaven.

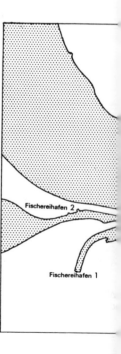

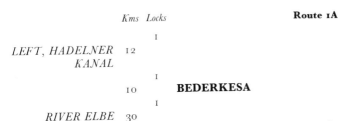

Kms	*Locks*	**Route 1A**
	I	
LEFT, HADELNER KANAL 12		
	I	
10		**BEDERKESA**
	I	
RIVER ELBE 30		

About 14kms down the coast from the huge
Otterndorf lock is:
CUXHAVEN. Each of the three basins can be entered
at any state of the tide; they are, from NE, Alter
Hafen, Fischerei Hafen and Amerika Hafen and there
are inner basins but the first named offers the best
chance of a berth. The Aussen Hafen is used by
yachts waiting for the tide but it is exposed and can be
most uncomfortable. A yacht haven has been planned
here for some time.
Cuxhaven is an important fishing harbour and is
developing as a seaside resort: the sandy beach,
though narrow is attractively situated with a grassy
strip and the promenade behind from which many
view the frequent passage of big ships.
(Connect Route 3)

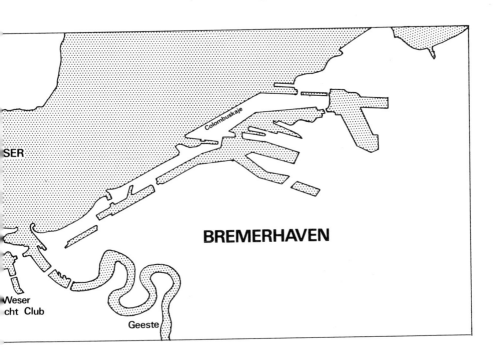

Route 2 **Brunsbüttelkoog to Kiel**

The NORD-OSTSEE KANAL, or the KIEL CANAL, links the North Sea and the Baltic, thus its name, North Sea-East Sea Canal.

The canal was opened by Wilhelm II in 1895 and it was previously known as the Kaiser Wilhelm Kanal. The completion of the canal enabled the German Battle Fleet to move quickly from the Baltic to the North Sea.

The five iron bridges over it are 42m high. The shipping passing through, (averaging one every eight minutes every day and night of the year), is a major tourist attraction, particularly at the locks at each end, Brunsbüttelkoog and Holtenau; the larger of the pair of each of these locks can take ships of 330m length, 45m beam, 14m draft and 40m height above water level. Within these locks there are harbours and in the Brunsbüttel harbour a number of yachts are kept.

With a length of about 100kms and a speed limit of 8 knots the passage straight through the canal, including locking in and out, takes about eight hours. No stopping is allowed in the canal but you can turn out of the canal into the small haven at Burgerauhafen, Km. 17, into the Gieslau Kanal at Km. 40, to Obereidersee at Km. 66, to Borgstedt at Km. 70

The Kiel Canal.

and to the Seglerbrücke at Km. 98.5. Distances are marked in kilometres from the Brunsbüttel end. There are eleven passing places for ships over 6,000GRT or 6ml draft. The canal is lighted and is open day and night but yachts are not allowed to move through at night; they must so time their passage that they either pass through the canal in daylight or are secured out of the canal in one of the stopping places mentioned above before dark. In fog or bad visibility yachts must stop out of the way and can use the inner side of the big ship moorings in canal sidings.

But after dark yachts can lock IN to the Brunsbüttel yacht harbour and OUT of Holtenau lock.

Every vessel using the canal must have onboard a copy of the Canal Regulations, *Betriebsordnung für den Nord-Ostsee Kanal*. Extracts from a *translation* of these regulations are given in Appendix III of the North Sea Pilot IV, (No. 55), and these *extracts* alone run to twenty-six pages but, of course, the Betriesordnung relates to big ships and an extract applying to vessels up to 50 tons, (GRT), is available from the canal offices or German yachting association, DSV, or Automobile Club, ADAC. English versions are available.

Some of the points covered by this extract have already been dealt with. Perhaps one of the most important is the inner signal pattern which indicates which position in which lock you proceed to. If it is all beyond you you need not worry for since this is the busiest canal section in the world there is always somebody going your way whom you can follow. You get moving on the outer signals of flashing green over flashing red which brings you to the inner signals which will give you greens and whites and reds and whites, all flashing. On greens you go to the LEFT lock and on reds you go to the RIGHT lock, (the opposite to your navigation lights). That at least gets you into the correct lock chamber. If the signal pattern showed two coloured you would go to the outside wall of the lock and if it showed one coloured you would go to the inside wall.

The same signal patterns are at Brunsbüttel and Holtenau. To simplify any confusion that might be in your mind or to hurry you up, any other qualifying instructions would come over the loud speaker system to you probably in English—so many British ships pass through and many languages are heard.

Once in, you go to the lock offices to pay, and keep the receipt to show to lock officials at either end.

A sailing yacht is not allowed to sail through the canal. If you have an engine (going) you can have your sails up but you must not tack because, understandably, you must keep well out of the way of the big ships, in fact a distance of 10–15m from your starboard bank. What really is good advice is to be most watchful when being passed by big ships because the undertow, if you happen to be too near, can be frightening and there is nothing you can do once you are being drawn into the warehouse-size side of a passing ship. You really must keep as far out of the way as you can because ships cannot flick their wheel to dodge around you as a lorry around a cyclist. I have mentioned in other books what an enlightening experience it would be for some yachtsmen to stand on the bridge of a ship when passing through yacht infested waters.

From the Brunsbüttel end it so happens that every stopping place in the canal is on the opposite bank and you must take great care when crossing the fairway.

One yacht may even tow another through the canal if the combined GRT is less than 50, provided that both helms are manned and that it is possible to maintain about 10kms per hour.

There are sidings in the canal for big ships and the signals of these you may ignore unless they happen to show three flashing red in which case you must stop.

Route 2

Distance	103 kms
Number of locks	2
Minimum height above water	40m
Minimum depth of water	2m 70

	Km	*Locks*	
	Mark		
NORD-OSTSEE	00	I	**BRUNSBÜTTELKOOG.** The Elbe end of the Kiel
KANAL			Canal. The principal attraction of this town is ships, ships and more ships of all nationalities, shapes and sizes, a seemingly never ending procession day and night. There is a harbour inside the lock gates which is convenient should you wish to relax before embarking on the passage of the canal. As already mentioned you are not allowed to stop in the canal but there are one or two diversions for smaller ships.
	17		**BURG HAFEN**
(L. Gieselau Kanal and River Eider)	40		

— — — — — — — — — — — — — — — — — — — —

a diversion from the KIEL CANAL to TONNING on the North Sea:

Distance	52 kms
Number of locks	3
Minimum height above water	4m 2
Minimum depth of water	1m 5

GIESELAU KANAL			
		I	
STR. ON RIVER EIDER			
(R. River Eider to Rendsburg)			
		2	
	36		**FRIEDRICHSTADT.** At the junction of the Treene

Route 2

and the Eider; the harbour is reached from the lock from the Eider.

14   **TONNING**

NORTH SEA

Tonning.

NORD-OSTSEE 66   **RENDSBURG.** Most famous, probably, for the
KANAL   Eisenbahnhochbrüche, the railway bridge that
crosses the canal at a height of 42m, with a
transporter bridge slung below the metal framework.
There is also a road tunnel underneath the canal for
cars and pedestrians.

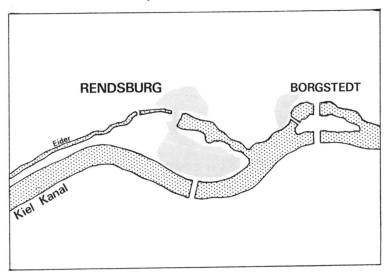

Rendsburg.

Route 2

| NORD-OSTEE KANAL | Km Mark | Locks | The Port of Rendsburg provides a convenient berth |

NORD-OSTEE KANAL   *Km* *Locks*   *Mark*

The Port of Rendsburg provides a convenient berth away from the restless canal. Beyond the wharves it is an attractive old town with an enormous esplanade. The opening of the canal created industrial development; the old town of Rendsburg was once on an island in the Eider and the Eider was once a frontier between Schleswig and Holstein. The waterfront is pleasant, a tree-lined grandstand from which to watch the shipping procession. The Eider is sealed off in Rendsburg so that it is not possible to cruise from here to join the Gieselau Kanal along the Eider.

70   **BORGSTEDT**

98   I   **HOLTENAU**

Holtenau.

Kms Locks   **Route 2**

KIELER FORDE   5   **KIEL.** In addition to the fame of the canal often named after it, Kiel has established a world reputation as a yachting Mecca for its KIEL WEEK in June, an event that has taken place for the last eighty years. The Olympic Games have also had a considerable influence on yachting facilities here. On locking out of the Holtenau lock you turn to starboard into the Kieler Hafen, past the moorings at Wik that are too small to be of interest to the cruising yacht, and you will then see moorings to starboard, at Düsternbrook, the yacht club hafen with all facilities being just on the bend. The opposite shore of the hafen is devoted to ship-building. If you

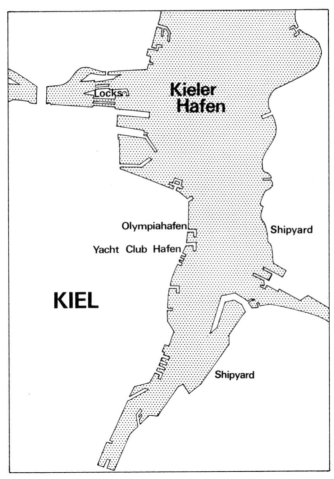

Laboe

Kiel (cont.)   **Route 2**

are proceeding through Kieler Förde on leaving the
Holtenau Lock, having turned to port you will then
find a pleasant little harbour to starboard at Laboe,
distinguished by the Naval Memorial Monument
where there is also a shipping museum; but watch
your echo sounder here.

Further up to port you will come to the biggest
yacht harbour of Kiel-Schilksee that was constructed
for the 1972 Olympic Games and has everything you

Kiel-Schilksee, Olympic Games harbour.

Kiel (cont.)

could wish for in a yacht harbour although somewhat remote; but there is a bus service to Kiel.

Just above Kiel-Schilksee is the pleasant little yacht harbour of Strande and 25kms or so further on 'round the corner' the yacht harbour and holiday resort of Eckernförde.

Opposite the Holtenau lock is Möltenort, a small fishing harbour but with yachting facilities.

Kiel, at the end of a fjord 10kms long, is an ideal natural harbour. It was totally destroyed in WW2, including the 17thC university and the old castle. It is now a modern town of broad streets and squares, parks and shopping precincts.

Kiel.

Route 3 **Cuxhaven to Lauenberg**

Distance	156 kms
Number of locks	1
Minimum height above water	unlimited
Minimum depth of water	5m (tidal)

Kms

RIVER ELBE   **CUXHAFEN**
                     (Connect Route 1A)

(R. Otterndorf 14
      entrance to
Hadelner Kanal)

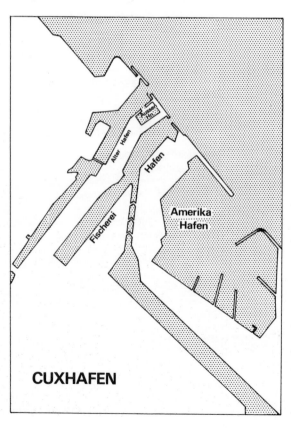

CUXHAFEN

RIVER ELBE	*Kms*	**Route 3**
(R. Die Oste navigable for 65kms to Bremervörde, depth 1m1 at high water)	7	
(L. Nord-Ostsee Kanal)	11	
(L. Stör to Itzehoe, 21kms, least depth 3m)	18	
(L. Die Rhin)	4	**GLUCKSTADT.** There is a small harbour.
(R. Schwinge)	22	
	12	**WEDEL.** A splendid yachthaven, in fact there are two yachthavens here, the larger being the one to port; the Customs and Police are in the other. It is convenient to sort out 'your papers' here, also duty free fuel but apart from this there are no attractions apart from a small cafe ashore. It is about a mile to the town of Wedel from where you can take the underground, (overground), into Hamburg.
	1	**SCHULAU.** There is a smaller yachthaven here.
	21	**HAMBURG.** This is the largest seaport in Germany

Hamburg in the largest seaport in Germany.

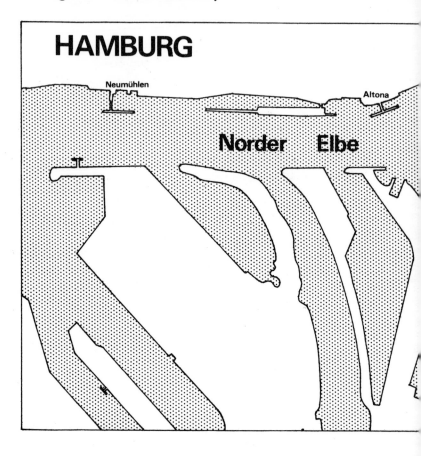

Route 3

RIVER ELBE

with twenty-five miles of quays and big ships parked everywhere. After the petrol refineries to starboard you come to what appears to be a waterway maze to starboard, (with a rise and fall of less than 2m50 there are no locks to the majority of basins). Proceed ahead into the Norder Elbe, dodging ferries from the Neumühlen, Altoni and St. Pauli landing stages after which the river bends slightly to the right where you can turn in to port to the Binnenhafen. There are many canals to explore and many possible moorings but take careful note of the tidal situation before leaving your craft. If you are anxiously seeking a mooring towards the end of the day it would be best to put in at Wedel but with plenty of time and light you will find a place to secure in the Binnenhafen area. Tides will not worry you once you

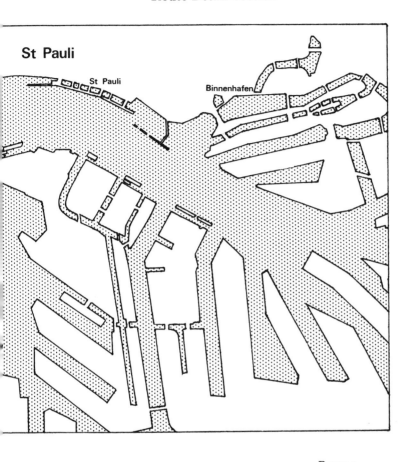

St Pauli

St Pauli

Binnenhafen

Route 3

RIVER ELBE

become submerged in the night life of Hamburg. It is said to resemble Venice; the number of canals is certainly bewildering and a lot of Hamburg is built on piles. But here the resemblance ends. The ebb and flow of the Elbe with assistance from the Alster and the Binnen Alster basin right in the old city are special to Hamburg. The night life certainly is. From the Binnenhafen the neon jungle of St. Pauli is only a short walk away; here are hundreds of bars, music, noise and the famous or infamous Reeperbahn. During the day there are museums, art galleries, splendid shops. Hamburg is a modern city since more than half of it was destroyed in WW2. The River Elbe is tidal for about 35kms above Hamburg, up to the lock at Geesthacht.

RIVER ELBE	Kms	Locks	Route 3
(R. River Ilmenau to Luneberg, least depth 1m10)	20		
		I	
(R. the new Elbe-Seiten Kanal will branch off here)	20		
	6		**LAUENBURG.**

LAUENBURG. A pleasant town of half-timbered houses at the junction of the Elbe and the Lübeck-Elbe Canal. Shipping from behind the Iron Curtain is more noticeable above Hamburg. The Elbe borders the Peoples' Republic from here and you can see the grim frontier and the watch towers. The Elbe passes beyond the Iron Curtain at Cumlosen.
(Connect Routes 10, 14)

Route 4 **Duisburg to Dortmund**

Distance	58 kms
Number of locks	7
Minimum height above water	4m 25
Minimum depth of water	2m 50

Locks

RHEIN-HERNE KANAL

DUISBURG. Above the river the chimneys wave their fiendish flags of smoke, purple and ochre from blast furnace and chemical works. Apart from—or because of—the industry of coal, iron, (greatest producer in the country), and steel, (produces nearly half of Germany's crude steel), this is the largest inland port in the world with thirty miles of quays and every conceivable facility for handling every conceivable type of cargo.

Duisburg and Ruhrort are connected. If a cruising yacht wished to secure here the best chance of a mooring is to port by the Ebert bridge.

Weaving your way across the Rhine the prospect ahead of waterways and basins is confusing and, of course, you feel a little out of place obviously bent on pleasure amongst every other vessel in working clothes. But the flow of traffic is a guide and you soon find yourself at the Duisburg-Meiderich lock.

1

From this point the canal does not pass through any towns but near to
OBERHAUSEN

Towards Oberhausen.

| | *Kms* | *Locks* | **Route 4** |

RHEIN-HERNE
KANAL

GELSENKIRCHEN
WANNE-EICKEL
HERNE
CASTROP-RAUXEL and

5   RECKLINGHAUSEN

There are so many factories and works that the built up area is continuous. Coal mine and slag heap, blast furnace and rolling mill, sulphuric acid and chemical manufacture, all the most hideously industrial sights have been concentrated here, blackening the water and polluting the air, squeezing out nature utterly.

But trees appear by RECKLINGHAUSEN where you turn right into the Schiffshebewerk, the canal-lift in that part of the Dortmund-Ems Kanal leading down to

RIGHT,
DORTMUND-EMS
KANAL

I

58   **DORTMUND.** The largest city of Westphalia and the capital of beer; having come through such grime and smoke you can understand the need for vast quantities of beer. Dortmund is a steel town too but is mainly concerned with sugar and wheat.

The harbour area is large and industrial as you would expect.

Route 4A **Duisburg to Essen**

Distance	40 kms
Number of locks	6
Minimum height above water	3m 15
Minimum depth of water	1m 80

	Kms	Locks	
RIVER RUHR			**DUISBURG**
			(Connect Routes 4, 11)
		6	
	40		**ESSEN**

this route leads nowhere else and since it is wholly industrial it is of no interest to the cruising yachtsman.

. . . yachtsman's nightmare . . . Duisburg.

Route 5 **Elsfleth to Dorpen**

Distance	91 kms
Number of locks	2
Minimum height above water	4m
Minimum depth of water	2m 20 (part tidal)

	Kms	Locks	
RIVER WESER			**ELSFLETH** *(Connect Route 1)*
RIGHT, RIVER *HUNTE (tidal)*			
	22		**OLDENBURG.** You are in company with small ships coming up here on top of the tide. This is a pleasant town of market gardening and flower growing, also renowned as the centre of Stone Age country where the giants' beds, or Hünenbetten are found. South of Oldenburg is the Visbecker Bridegroom, 360ft long, known as Germany's Stonehenge. St. Lambert's ch. 13thC.
CONTINUE AS *KÜSTEN KANAL*		1	
	18		**EDEWECHT**
(R. Elisabethfehn *Kanal to Leer, 4* *locks, depth 1m)* *(Connect Route 6)*			
	27		**ESTERWEGEN**
LEFT RIVER EMS		1	
	24		**DORPEN** *(Connect Route 6)*

Route 6 **Emden to Datteln**

Distance	246 kms
Number of locks	17
Minimum height above water	4m 25
Minimum depth of water	2m 50

Kms Locks

RIVER EMS

EMDEN. The sound signal 'code' for requesting entry to the harbour of your choice is shown in the Pilot. You can enter at any state of the tide. It is of course, a commercial harbour but if you proceed straight ahead through the Binnenhafen as far as you can (subject to the opening of the railway bridge) making for the tall Rathaus with what appears to be a giant egg-timer on its roof above the clock you will find a very pleasant little harbour quay opposite the Rathaus. Flowers will be visible through the saloon windows and you will not see the iron ore that is being shipped beyond. From this quay you can join the Dortmund-Ems canal by cruising back through the Binnenhafen but turning to port to the Industrie Hafen at the end of which is the canal. East Frisian Museum, (in the Rathaus): 16thC arms and armour.
(Connect Route 18)

(L. River Leda)   28

LEER. Turn in to the River Leda to port out of the Ems after the first bridge over, and again to port to the lock into the attractive harbour of Leer. You can secure in the centre of this pleasant little town; it is a picturesque inland port with a noted cattle market.
(Connect Route 5)

I

17   **PAPENBURG**

CONTINUE AS
DORTMUND-EMS
KANAL

	Kms	*Locks*	**Route 6**
DORTMUND-EMS *KANAL* *(L. Küsten-kanal* *Connect Route 5)*	20		
		2	
	2		**DORPEN** *(Connect Route 5)*
		1	
	9		**LATHEN**
		1	
(R. Haren-Rüten *Kanal)*	12		**HAREN**
		1	
	13		**MEPPEN**
(L. Hase, R. Ems)		2	
	22		**LINGEN**
		1	
(R. Ems)			
(R. Ems-Vecht Kanal)			
(R. Ems)			
		7	
(L. Mittelland-Kanal)	35		
	11		**IBBENBÜREN**
		1	
	33		**MÜNSTER.** Capital of Westphalia. The Peace of Westphalia, 24 Oct 1648, which ended the Thirty Years War was signed here; portraits of the signatories can be seen in the Peace Hall of the Rathaus. This and other historic buildings have been reconstructed after WW2 damage, the Prinzipalmarkt particularly, the main arcaded street of Renaissance houses. Cathedral 13thC.
	15		**SENDEN**
	13		**LÜDINGHAUSEN**
(R. Wesel-Datteln *Kanal)*			

Münster

	Kms	**Route 6**

DORTMUND-EMS 16
KANAL

DATTELN. Almost at the cross 'roads' of the Wesel-Datteln, Dortmund-Ems and Rhein-Herne canals.

(Connect Route 17)

Route 7 **Koblenz to Laasphe**

Distance	224 kms
Number of locks	19
Minimum height above water	3m 20
Minimum depth of water	1m 6

As usual commercial shipping has priority over yachts on the beautiful River Lahn, but this priority is more urgent on the Lahn because larger vessels manoeuvre with difficulty in the narrow sections and in the tide; the approach channels to some of the locks on this river are very narrow, and yachts must be prepared to get out of the way smartly.
You can pay one fee for all the locks at the Niederlahnstein lock. The locks are open from 06.00 to 20.00 on weekdays and 09.00 to 18.00 on Sundays and holidays.
Speed limits are shown.
You can get fuel most conveniently at Nievern before the Strassenbrück to port; at Bad Ems to port behind the bridge; to starboard by the road bridge at Nassau; in Balduinstein in front of the bridge to port; at Diez to port behind the second road bridge.

	Km Mark	Locks	
RHEIN			**KOBLENZ** *(Connect Routes 8, 9, 11)*
	585		
LEFT, Rhein			
RIVER LAHN	137 Lahn		**LAHNSTEIN.** Divided by the River Lahn into NIEDERLAHNSTEIN and
	136		OBERLAHNSTEIN above which is Lahneck Castle. From the pentagonal tower you can see the way ahead into the Lahn valley.
		2	
	132		**AHL.** In a pleasant country setting.
	128		**NIEVERN.** The scene is industrial here.
		2	
			BAD EMS. The approach to Bad Ems is impressively beautiful and the quay-promenade excites the prospect of a most attractive mooring; but check carefully before coming alongside because there is insufficient depth by most of the quay since it is not dredged and the main channel is on the opposite side of the fairway. A hundred years ago Bad Ems was a fashionable spa and Kaiser Wilhelm used to take the cure here as a monument testifies. There is also a plaque on the quay, dated July 1870, recalling the request of the French Ambassador, Benedetti, to Wilhelm to renounce claims to the Spanish throne.

Km Mark	Locks	Route 7
RIVER LAHN		The refusal of Wilhelm started a chain of events that brought about the Franco-Prussian War.
120	1	**DAUSENAU**
116	1	**NASSAU.** A health resort but principally famous for the castle of the House of Orange-Nassau, now the reigning dynasty of Holland; and not forgetting William of Orange, William III of England.
110	2	**OBERNHOF.** A small village of half-timbered houses.
102	1	**LAURENBURG**
94	1	**GEILNAU**

Dausenau.

	Km *Locks* *Mark*	Route 7
RIVER LAHN	91	**BALDUINSTEIN.** There are famous castle ruins here.
	86	**FACHINGEN**
	83	**DIEZ.** There is a small harbour in this pleasant town of timbered houses.
	76 (2)	**LIMBURG.** An attractive town of half-timbered houses. From afar you see the beautiful Romanesque Cathedral.
	73	**DIETKIRCHEN**
	71	**DEHRN**

LAHN CANAL

Pay particular attention to your echo sounder from here—regarded as the limit for 250 ton barges.

	65 (1)	**RUNKEL.** An old village dominated by its castle, the best view of which is from the river as you approach the old village. One of the most attractive situations in this attractive valley of the Lahn.
	62 (1)	**VILLMAR**
	59	**ARFURT**
	54	**AUMENAU**
	49 (1)	**GRÄVENECK**

TUNNEL (2)

	39	**WEILBURG.** A most picturesque old town with a splendid castle and gardens. Museum of the House of Nassau.
	30 (1)	**BISKIRCHEN**
	24	**BRAUNFELS.** Dominated by its castle high above you from the river.
	11	**WETZLAR.** A Cathedral town at the junction of the rivers Dill and Lahn. Goethe's association with Charlotte took place here but today it is known as the birthplace of the 35mm film and the home of the Leica camera. Lotte's House: Furniture and mementoes of Charlotte and first editions of Werther.

Limburg.

Km
Mark
                                      Route 7

LAHN   o   **DUTENHOFEN**
This is the navigable limit with a least depth of 1m6. New kilometre marking starts. It is said that Cölbe can be reached at half-tide and Laasphe at highwater but we have not attempted it.

    6   **GIESSEN.** A university town.

   39   **MARBURG.** A most famous university town, founded 1527. Above the twisting terraced streets and alleys of half-timbered houses stands Marburg Castle. St. Elisabeth ch. 13thC.

   43   **COLBE**

   87   **LAASPHE**

Koblenz.

Route 8 **Koblenz to Rheinfelden**

Distance	442 kms
Number of locks	12
Minimum height above water	4m 15
Minimum depth of water	1m 70

Km
Mark

RIVER RHEIN 591

KOBLENZ. Meeting point of three rivers, the Rhine, Moselle and Lahn, the history of Koblenz goes back two thousand years. Many historically important buildings have been reconstructed after WW2 damage which destroyed 85 per cent of the city. The corner of the junction of the Rhine and Moselle is Deutsches Eck; once there was a vast equestrian statue of Wilhelm I here but now only the base remains and there are over one hundred steps to the top of this. Another famous landmark is the fortress of Ehrenbreitstein high up on the opposite bank of the Rhine and floodlit at night. The most congenial mooring in Koblenz is on the Moselle side, on the port side before the beautiful Balduinbrücke.
The Weindorf is over on the Rhine side under the Pfaffendorfer bridge, a village of wine with tables and benches in the open and half-timbered wine houses around and lights in the trees and dancing. I first sampled the beautiful Rhine and Moselle wines here and staggered back to the boat past huge, striking flags draped from every building.
Koblenz is a most happy place of the most beautiful wine and the convivial atmosphere reaches its climax during the second week in August when the 'Rhine in Flames' festival is held.
(Connect Routes 7, 9, 11)

585

KAPELLAN-STOLZENFELS. Above the row of houses is the Castle of Stolzenfels, 13thC, restored 1825. For 60kms you will be surveyed from above by a great many castles, some spectacular.

(L. River Lahn) 584

LAHNSTEIN. Divided by the River Lahn into

| | *Km*
Mark | *Lahnstein (cont.)*   **Route 8** |

Niederlahnstein, on the nearest bank of the Lahn as you approach from Koblenz and Oberlahnstein where the harbour is. After the turmoil of the Rhine this can be quite a quiet refuge although both parts of the town are essentially industrial.

580   **BRAUBACH.** The Castle of Marksburg here is about the only Rhine castle that has never been destroyed.

575   **OSTERSPAI.** Above is the Castle of Liebeneck. In the spring the cherry blossom is a delight for this is in the fruit growing region.

570   **BOPPARD.** A beautiful little town of Celtic origin in a setting of vine covered hills, a favourite holiday resort with an attractive Rhine promenade. By the quay is the Gothic Carmelite church. From nearby you can take a chair lift to the well-known Vierseenplatz, (place of the four lakes), which gives you a view of four sections of the Rhine as it curves away but which look like four lakes. From here too you can feel the Rhine current becoming stronger.

567   **BORNHOFEN.** The Rhine Gorge begins at this point known as the Hostile Brothers, a legend associated with the castles of Liebenstein and Sterrenberg. The scenery is wilder and you are really feeling the power of the current now.
Between here and Bad Salzig you see the long tows of barges breaking up into smaller groups that the tugs can manage to haul up past Bingen; those barges left behind anchoring to await the return of the tug which has then left the first section of his tow anchored ahead. Some barges lighten load and draft by unloading part of their cargo.

556   **ST. GOAR.** You can pause to gather your confidence here for there is a harbour in this pleasant little resort that is associated with wine and named after the missionary/hermit who did his good deeds here 1500 years ago.
The Rhine signal stations now commence, pilots join and leave, and round the right-hand bend ahead is the Loreley where the passage of the Rhine narrows and the sheer rock rises 130m high, at its base the mysterious echo and on the rock itself the golden haired siren luring the cruising yachtsmen of folklore to their doom. To sometimes see rocks right in the

Boppard.

Km
Mark

Route 8

RIVER RHEIN

middle of the swift current beyond the Loreley is somewhat disconcerting but, when they are visible, the Rhine skippers use this Jungfrauen, the seven rocks, as tide gauges to check the level of the river as the rocks appear.

550   **OBERWESEL.** There is also a harbour here and much to see. The bold towers of the Castle of Schönburg above the pleasant walled town of Oberwesel, and ahead what at first appears to your astonished eye to be a 'KING GEORGE V' Class battleship but which turns out to be Die Pfalz, a Rhine stronghold built on an island in the river for the purpose of collecting tolls in the bad old days but now with signal yard-arms sticking out from either side of its roof.

With the throttle lever pushed as far as it will go and the engines taking on that specially injured note when they seem to be saying 'how long are you going to keep this up', you struggle to make barely 5kms in the hour over the ground. And the toughest reach, the Binger Loch, lies ahead.

No wonder you see tugs pirouetting in the swift current like benevolent vultures waiting for an eager prey, scanning you for a signal that you need their aid up through the rapids; no wonder that two hundred pilots are based on the little village of Kaub to guide vessels through just this small section of the Rhine.

543   **BACHARACH.** A picturesque small town of famous vineyards, dominated by the castle of Stahleck.

(L. River Wisper) 540   **LORCH.** A wine village with the ruins of the castle of Nollig above.

535   **TRECHTINGSHAUSEN.** By this ancient wine village with the spectacularly sited castle of Reichenstein above, you enter the dangerous rapids, taking the channel to port and guided by the buoys lying flat on their backs through the turmoil of the water. The separate channel to starboard is for defined UP going traffic like the big KÖLN-DÜSSELDORFERS and for DOWN traffic. Here is the notorious Binger Loch and the Mäuseturm, or Mouse Tower, simply a turreted-top, brown, upright oblong stuck on an island, small as a cardboard model by comparison with the ranging tiers of hills behind; the island forming part of the Binger Loch reef and the one time toll station of the Mäuseturm now with signal yard-arms poking from its turrets.

Die Pfalz—like meeting a battleship.

	Route 8

Km
RIVER RHEIN *Mark*
(R. River Nahe) 528   **BINGEN.** There is a harbour here and it is an important river port, therefore somewhat industrial. The bridge over the River Nahe stands on the same site as a former Roman bridge. Ahead the river broadens beyond the grip of the gorge.

527   **RÜDESHEIM.** You can begin to relax here and your overworked engines too. The worst is behind you and this is a pleasant holiday centre with dancing and song and wine bars. There is an aerial railway to the Niederwald monument and a wine museum in the fortified castle of Brömserburg.

511   **ELTVILLE.** Famous for wine and roses; there is cultivation on both banks and you are relieved to see the river banks spreading wider apart now although tufts of islands appear here and there in midstream.

505   **SCHIERSTEIN.** A small port surrounded by orchards and vineyards; but stand by to check your height under the bridge at the entrance.

498   **MAINZ.** At the confluence of the Rhine and Main this is the largest wine town in Germany. The harbour is industrial but not at all unpleasant. The town is pleasantly compact and from the Zollhafen it is not far to the cathedral, founded 9thC. In the Gutenberg Museum is Gutenberg's handpress and a Gutenberg Bible.

(L. River Main) 481   **NIERSTEIN.** The Niersteiner label is as famous as Bernkastel as the town does not hesitate to advertise. There are hundreds of vineyards here.

481   **OPPENHEIM.** There is a small harbour here and the vineyards are almost as good as Nierstein.

462   **GERNSHEIM.** An industrial harbour in an industrial area.

443   **WORMS.** One of the oldest towns in Germany. Your view of it from the cockpit is industrial, (but after the dramatic scenery of castles and the excitement of the gorge, the Rhine above Mainz is something of an anti-climax).
However, there is certainly a harbour at Worms, an industrial port in fact but it is a town rich in history as any schoolboy will tell you. The

Km	Locks	**Route 8**

RIVER RHEIN *Mark*

Liebfrauenstift vineyard is situated by the
Liebfrauen church; from here the name of
Liebfraumilch originated.
Worms Cathedral dates from the 11thC.
Luther Monument.

(L. River Neckar) 427   **MANNHEIM.** At the confluence of the Rhine and
Neckar this is the second largest river port in Germany
with miles of quays and harbour installations.
Turn in to port to the Mühlauhafen after the
entrance to the River Neckar.
Mannheim was laid out in the 17thC on a chess-
board or grid-iron pattern; within the area of the
Neckar and Rhine the streets parallel to the rivers
have letters and the cross streets are numbered.
Fine Arts Museum.
Reiss Museum
(Connect Route 13)

425   **LUDWIGSHAVEN.** An industrial town with
industrial wharves.

400   **SPEYER.** The largest Romanesque church, 11thC,
in Europe is here and the crypt is the burial place
of eight emperors. In the Wine Museum is the
world's oldest wine.
There is also a harbour. Speyer is a charming place.

384   **GERMERSHEIM.** An industrial town with a
harbour, once a Roman citadel.

360   **KARLSRUHE.** Another town built to a geometric
plan, in this case fan shaped.
Karlsruhe is an important inland harbour; on entry
you are faced with five separate basins. You are
likely to find the quays to port most congenial. A
city of imposing buildings, the commercial
atmosphere of Karlsruhe is relieved by splendid parks
and gardens.

354   **NEUBURG.** This is the French-German frontier
where you must report and there is a convenient
inlet to enable you to do so from here:

to starboard . . . Alsace, FRANCE
to port . . . Baden-Württenburg, GERMANY

and from here to Kehl the river current increases in
strength.

I

	Km	Locks Mark	Route 8

RIVER RHEIN
(R. Canal de la Marne   293
au Rhin and Rhône-Rhin
Canal at STRASBOURG)

KEHL (Germany). The inlet basins are quite extensive and considered to be the most convenient on the whole river since trains of barges can pull in and leave like railway trains at a station. As far back as the Middle Ages Kehl assumed importance as the place from which you crossed to Strasbourg; and then a bridge was built which was then the only fixed bridge from here to the mouth of the Rhine— between the free imperial city and the fishing village of Kehl.

Kehl obviously suffers by comparison with its sophisticated neighbour across the bridge and has no attractions ashore.

In 1956 Germany and France agreed on a partial canalisation scheme whereby the canal joined and rejoined the river, creating the barrages at Strasbourg, Gerstheim, Rhinau and Marckolsheim. In 1961 the big locks at Kembs and Niffer were built enabling big river vessels to proceed to the Rhine-Rhône-Canal, the Rhône and the Mediterranean.

RIVER RHEIN 225   4

BREISACH (Germany). Dominating the river is the rock of Breisach and its church. There is a good harbour and quay.

170   4

WEIL (Germany). A river port amidst the hills of the Black Forest.

The frontier with SWITZERLAND is here and there is a small 'bulge' of Switzerland on the river bank to port.

149   2

RHEINFELDEN. The start and finish of Rhine navigation. There is a town of Rheinfelden on each bank, one Swiss and one German. The German side offers the better mooring, the Swiss offers most attractions ashore—but there is a bridge.

1

Route 9 **Koblenz to Perl**

Distance	268 kms
Number of locks	12
Minimum height above water	3m 53
Minimum depth of water	2m 50

Km Locks
Mark (R) = right bank of the river, (L) = left

RIVER MOSEL   **KOBLENZ.** From your mooring on the port side of
(the construction   the Moselle before the beautiful Balduinbrücke,
of the locks and   the Balduin Bridge, proceed under the railway
dams that made   bridge and the Neue Moselbrücke to the Koblenz
the river   Lock. The factories and industry, you feel, should
navigable to   not have been allowed in such a beautiful place.
Luxembourg and
France was not   5   **GÜLS** (R). There is a small mooring here.
completed until
1964)   10   **WINNINGEN** (R). The place to be at the autumn
wine festival.

17   **KOBERN** (R). A pleasant little town overlooked by
ruins of Oberburg and Niederburg castles.
Roman tower.

       I

19   **GONDORF** (R). The huge castle dates from the
15thC.

24   **ALKEN** (L). Possesses a landing stage below its
towers and old walls.

25   **LÖF** (R). Alongside mooring is possible.

26   **BRODENBACH** (L). A pleasant village with a good
harbour. In the valley above are the ruins of
Ehrenburg Castle.

28   **HATZENPORT** (R). There is a small mooring by
the ferry tower.

34   **MOSELKERN** (R). At the foot of the Eltz valley.
Above is Eltz Castle, one of the most splendid in the
country.

Balduinbrücke bridge at
Koblenz on the river Mosel.

Km Locks Mark		Route 9

1

RIVER MOSEL   37   **MUDEN** (R)

39   **KARDEN** (R). There is a mooring in this one time Roman settlement and some interesting buildings including a 12thC church. Noted for Engelsporter wine.

40   **TREIS** (L). Linked by the bridge with Karden.

51   **COCHEM** (R). A beautiful town with a most attractive quay, market square and timbered houses. Many tourists come here and the shops reflect this.

Traben-Trarbach.

Km Locks	**Route 9**

RIVER MOSEL *Mark*

The castle on the hill above dominates the scene. The favourite wine is Pinner Kreuzberg.

I

59   **FANKEL** (L). The lock is amidst the life of the village of timbered houses.

61   **BEILSTEN** (L). Even amongst so many attractive villages Beilsten stands out as an especially beautiful little fortified market town with narrow medieval alleyways and small quaint houses. The castle is the Burg Metternich, one time home of the Chancellor of that name.

68   **SENHEIM** (L). There is a harbour here but the shore attractions do not compare with those of the neighbouring villages; the Rosenberg and Wahrsager wines are interesting.

72   **EDIGER** (R). A pretty place with walls dating back to the 14thC.

I

81   **ALF** (R). Lying beneath the Marienburg and Arras castles this is an agreeable little village with a harbour. The spa here was known to the Romans.

87   **ZELL** (L). With a pleasant quay and promenade Zell is famous as a wine growing town and equally famous for its former castle of the Elector of Trier.

94   **PÜNDERICH** (L). A colourful little market town of ancient streets.

97   **REIL** (R). A pleasant old village.

I

102   **ENKIRCH** (L). A village noted for its half-timbered houses, also noted for its cage in which offenders were punished in public.

107   **TRABEN-TRARBACH.** A big wine centre connected by a bridge, Traben and Trarbach are treated as one. There are mooring facilities and above are the ruins of Grevenburg Castle.

113   **KROV** (R). An attractive village of 17thC houses, famous for its Kroever Nacktarsch wine.

I

123   **ZELTINGEN** (L). A pleasant town of unique half-timbered houses and a big wine centre. Himmelreich

Km Locks
Mark

Route 9

RIVER MOSEL

Zeltingen (cont.)
and Steinmauer wines come from here.
From Zeltingen to Klüsserath are the most famous
wine villages. In this middle part of the German
Moselle the towering river banks have quick drying
soil that is practically pure slate and when the steep
inclines have a southerly exposure the conditions are
ideal for the Riesling vine. As you look up into the
vast green amphitheatre you see workers clinging like
flies to the steeper slopes and through the glasses
you see carts being dragged by ropes and winches.
You also see sun dials fixed to the rocks here and at
Wehlen.

125   **WEHLEN** (R). Wehlener is considered to rank with
Bernkasteler in the fine wine league, particularly
Wehlener Sonnenuhr and Nonnenburg.

. . . premier vineyard in the country . . . Bernkastel.

Km Locks Mark	Route 9

RIVER MOSEL 127   **GRAACH** (L). Graacher is as eminent a wine as that of neighbouring Wehlen.

130   **KUES** (R). There is a good harbour quay here in an attractive setting with the white and grey of the houses contrasting with the rich green of the rolling hills behind. The wines of Kues, although splendid, do not enjoy the reputation of the vineyards across the bridge at

130   **BERNKASTEL** (L). Here the river bank rises to over 700ft and extends for over 8kms; here at Bernkastel are the most famous wines of the Moselle, the Bernkasteler Doktor being, perhaps, the premier vineyard in the country. Bernkastel-Kues Wine Festivals take place in early September. The market square of Bernkastel is most attractive with half-timbered houses overlooked by Landshut Castle.

138   **BRAUNEBERG** (L). Noted for its splendid Brauneberg Juffer wine.

139   **KESTEN** (R). Herrenberg is the wine of this pleasant village.

147   **PIESPORT** (L). A pretty village and one time Roman settlement. Piesporter Goldtröpfchen is justifiably one of the most famous wines in the world. The newer Piesport Gunterslay from the other side of the river does not enjoy the same reputation.

151   **DHRON** (L). Dhronhofberger is also a famous wine.

153   **NEUMAGEN** (L). A pleasant stop, best known for the discoveries here of Roman remains that are now in the Wine Museum at Trier.

156   **TRITTENHEIM** (R). There are alongside moorings here.

162   **KLÜSSERATH** (R). The wines from this slope go under the famous name of Bruderschaft; famous, too, is the castle.

166   **DETZEM** (L). Once a Celtic settlement and now well known for the beautiful Maximin-Klosterlay produced here.

	Km Mark	*Locks*
		I
RIVER MOSEL	169	

PÖLICH (R). A village with moorings in an especially beautiful situation.

174 **MEHRING** (R). A village with two interesting churches.

176 **LONGUICH** (R). Connected with Loersch-Longen by the bridge.

179 **SCHWEICH** (R). There are moorings in this beautiful wooded setting, also an 18thC ferry tower.

(L. River Ruwer, not navigable)

192 **TRIER** (L). The oldest city in Germany, said to have been founded in 15 BC. The Saar and the

Trier.

k ms	Locks	Route 9
RIVER MOSEL		Ruwer flow into the Moselle near here. Trier was a northern capital of Rome in the 4thC and is now the commercial wine centre for the Mosel-Saar-Ruwer wine district. There are conducted tours of wine cellars with the attraction of wine tasting, also the Mosel Wine Museum. The nearby commercial quays are not very convenient unfortunately.
(L. fork River Saar		Romanesque cathedral 14thC.
not navigable		Porta Nigra; Imperial Thermae.
here)	I	
		from here:
		to starboard . . . LUXEMBOURG
		to port . . . GERMANY
(R. River Sûre)	14	**WASSERBILLIG** (Luxembourg). There is a splendid quay here on the Moselle and another on the River Sûre. Wasserbillig is the frontier post from Luxembourg-Germany to Germany.
	4	**MERTERT** (Luxembourg). The River Syr flows into the Moselle here; there are quays and industry and not much charm.
	6 / I	**GREVENMACHER** (Luxembourg). Capital of the Luxembourg Moselle and centre of the wine district. You can visit the Bernard-Massard wine cellars. There are good mooring facilities but not a great deal of interest.
	14	**WORMELDANGE** (Luxembourg). Capital of the Riesling. A bridge crosses the Moselle here and there are quays.
	5	**EHNEN** (Luxembourg). An attractive village of medieval character with an unusual circular church.
	10 / I	**STADTBREDIMUS** (Luxembourg). A wine centre and a pleasant small village with a quay and a castle.
	6	**REMICH** (Luxembourg). St. Martin Wine Cellars are a big attraction in this pleasant little town that calls itself the 'Pearl of the Moselle'. The tree-lined promenade and quay by the bridge is most attractive and it is a very convenient berth.
	17	**PERL** (Germany). The last village in Germany on the Moselle. The Customs posts are by the lock.
	I	

Route 10 **Lauenburg to Fallers-Leben (near)**

THE ELBE-SEITEN KANAL

This new canal joins Hamburg and Lübeck to the western European waterway system. It might be supposed that this canal was built to avoid the deviation into East Germany that an inland voyage from Hamburg/Lübeck to the Mittelland Kanal now entails; in fact a link between the Elbe and the Mittelland Kanal was planned by a Prussian committee in 1930; to be known as the HANSA CANAL this was to run from the Elbe at Hamburg-Harburg, cross the Weser south of Bremen at Achim and connect with the Mittelland Canal at Bramsche, a distance of 200kms.

The new Elbe-Seiten Kanal is 115kms long and runs from Artlenburg on the Elbe to the upper part of the Mittelland Canal west of the Sülfield lock. The differences in height of water levels of 23m and 38m have been dealt with by the construction of a lock south of Uelzen and a double-lift north-east of Lüneburg.

Lüneberger Heide, or Luneberger Heath, is one of the most ancient lands of Germany where pre-historic man lived. We remember it perhaps as the place where Montgomery parked his caravan and the German High Command came to surrender in May 1945.

The construction of the Elbe-Seiten Canal began in May 1968 and took ten years to complete.

Distance	123 kms
Number of locks	2
Minimum depth of water	4m

	Kms	Locks	
RIVER ELBE			**LAUENBURG.** A town in a pleasant wooded setting with old sailor's houses on the site of a former castle. At one time there was much more river traffic here when the salt trade between Lauenburg and Lübeck was at its height. *(Connect Routes 3, 14)*
LEFT, INTO ELBE-SEITEN KANAL	7		**ARTLENBURG**
		1	
	50		**UELZEN**
		1	
	65		

Kms

LEFT, INTO
MITTELLAND
KANAL
(by Sülfield Lock)   1   **FALLERS-LEBEN**
(Connect Route 15)

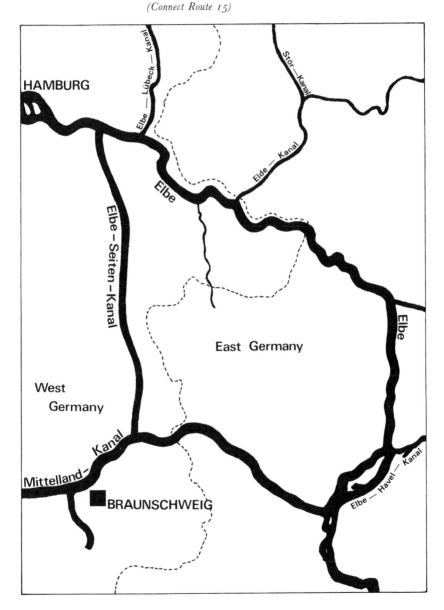

Route 11 **Lobith Dutch/German border to Koblenz**

Distance	271 kms
Number of locks	0
Minimum height above water	9m
Minimum depth of water	2m 10

RIVER RHEIN 862   **LOBITH** (Holland). A place of Customs activity for traffic DOWN the Rhine and since ships have been stopping here for many years, trading activities have developed to service them. Launches are continually fussing around ships anchored in the stream.

853   **EMMERICH.** A place of Customs activity for traffic UP the Rhine and of other trading activity as at Lobith. There is a harbour conveniently situated to enable you to report your presence in Germany which, obviously, you must do. Hundreds of ships each day hoist the green Customs flag here and the Customs may go out or the ships' boats may come in.

RIVER RHEIN

Emmerich is quite a pleasant town with an interesting Rhine Museum of model boats, old Rhine charts, views, history and folklore. St. Martin's cathedral.

837   **REES**

814   **WESEL.** Formerly a Hanseatic League town Wesel was destroyed in WW2 and is now a modern market town with a useful harbour. The Schill Museum is a memorial to eleven Schill officers who were shot in September 1809 on the orders of Napoleon. Lipperhey, inventor of the telescope, was born here. The bridge above you, crossing the river to Büderich, is the longest bridge on the Rhine. From Büderich the Allies crossed the Rhine in 1945.
(Connect Route 17)

	Km Mark	Route 11

(L. Wesel-Datteln Kanal)

793   **WALSUM.** The Rhine scene is rapidly becoming more industrialised from here and Walsum is a coal port handling the output of the mines of nearby Oberhausen.

760–   **DUISBURG-RUHRORT**
789   *(Connect Route 4)*

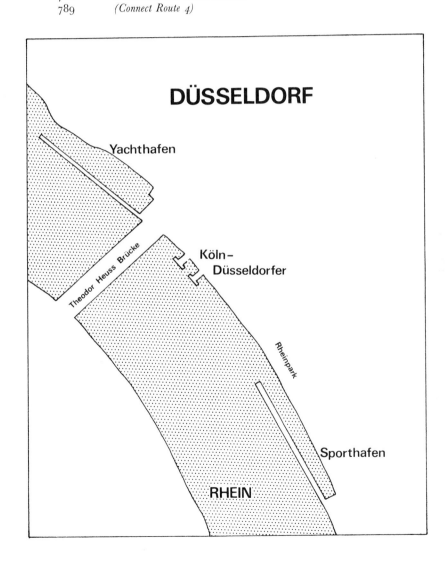

| | *Km* *Locks* | **Route 11** |
| | *Mark* | |

RIVER RHEIN 774   **RHEINHAUSEN.** Chimneys, blast furnaces and factories proclaim that this is the steel town of the area.

765   **KREFELD-UERDINGEN.** A centre of the silk, velvet and fashion industry.

743   **DÜSSELDORF.** Düsseldorf sounds industrial and is but there is a great deal of interest here as well; in fact the First Class Rhine Cruise Ships make a stop here.

Just before the first bridge, the Theodor-Heuss Brücke, you will see the Yachthafen. The port is just beyond the Kniebrücke, the third bridge. You need to take a deep breath to even contemplate the staggering variety of attractions. Seventeen museums cover the subjects of Glass, 20thC art, (Paul Klee collection), Natural History, Goethe, Photography, Old Düsseldorf, Ethnological, Animals and Birds, Meissen porcelain, Late Baroque Architecture; several art galleries, Ceramic Art, Industry and Commerce. Plus several theatres, the Düsseldorf Playhouse and the Opera House. Open-air chess, polo, horse-racing, golf, ice skating, parks and a zoo, aquarium. Trade Fairs, Festivals, castles, walking tours.

There are elegant boulevard cafes and shops—the 'Ko' is one of the most beautiful shopping thoroughfares in Europe—highly individual night clubs and real beer.

740   **NEUSS.** Opposite Düsseldorf, turning in under the Kniebrücke, is the canal and inland port of Neuss, industrial but with an important late Romanesque cathedral.

717   **ZONS.** A unique and delightful fortified medieval village.

705   **HITDORF.** There is quite a pleasant harbour here.

688   **KÖLN (COLOGNE).** Pass under four bridges and after the fourth, the one after the railway bridge (over which a thousand trains pass every day), close the shore and proceed into the Rheinauhafen. Köln is over two thousand years old. The 1stC AD wall is preserved in many parts and you can also see a Roman tower, Roman sewers, Roman gate and

Km   **Route 11**

RIVER RHEIN *Mark*

aqueduct, mosaic floors and unique Roman glass-
ware in the Romano–Germanic Museum. It took
over six hundred years to build Köln Cathedral, the
foundation stone having been laid in 1284. The best
view of it is from the Rhine Park on the other side of
the river which you can reach by cable railway high
over the Rhine, the only cable railway across a river
in Europe. You need a guide book to learn of the
treasures in the cathedral.

There are many old churches, a Motor Museum,
Eau de Cologne Museum, Lacquerwork Museum,
seven civic museums, art gallery, opera house and
municipal theatre, parks, game reserves, botanical
gardens and a zoo.

Hohe Strasse is the most famous street of shops.
There are many beer houses, some 15thC and a big
selection of night clubs.

655   **BONN.** Federal capital of Western Germany, a
temporary capital it is felt until the day when

. . . the capital, Bonn.

Km
Mark

Route 11

RIVER RHEIN

Berlin once more assumes the role. You can see the famous 'Old Tollhouse' and Beethovenhalle without coming ashore and indeed you would have a job to do so since the Köln–Düsseldorfer landing stage by the Kennedy Bridge is about the only mooring possibility here. But across the river upstream you will see yachts moored in behind the island at Bad Honnef.

645

KÖNIGSWINTER. A pleasant resort of riverside gardens, restaurants, horse-drawn carriages and pleasure boats. A resort that probably owes a lot of its tourist popularity to the Drachenfels, Germany's most frequently conquered mountain peak that dominates the town. You can ascend the 1,000ft peak in twenty minutes by rack railway and from the terrace it is fascinating and instructive to watch the procession of Rhine shipping below, for by comparison with the speedy downstream traffic the struggling upstream ships look almost stationary.

641

BAD HONNEF. As already mentioned there are moorings in behind the island here. The modern spa claims that it is in a particularly healthy situation and at least one neighbour could have testified to a healthy longevity for the villa of Conrad Adenauer was at nearby Rhöndorf.

638

OBERWINTER. An inlet port with yachting activity but ashore the village is simply one main street.

633

REMAGEN. The remains of the bridge you see, with St. Apollinaris church in the background, was the the Ludendorff Bridge that was mined prior to the American crossing of 7 March 1945 but the mines failed to go off; some time after the Americans had successfully completed their objective the bridge collapsed and, as you can see, it has not been rebuilt.

(From R.
River Ahr)

624

BAD HÖNNINGEN. On the hill behind is the Castle of Arenfels, said to have as many windows as there are days in the year.

623

BAD BREISIG

| | *Km* | **Route 11** |
| | *Mark* | |

RIVER RHEIN 620   **BROHL.** The little harbour here ships stone from the quarries in the Brohl valley and also specialises in timber and mineral water.

613   **ANDERNACH.** An industrial town.

592   **EHRENBREITSTEIN.** The fortress was built by the Prussians around 1820, the previous building having been destroyed by the French. A chair lift takes you up to the fortress in which the Central Rhine Museum is now situated.

591   **KOBLENZ**
(Connect Routes 7, 8, 9)

Route 12 **Mainz to Nürnberg**

Distance	464 kms
Number of locks	44
Minimum height above water	4m 68
Minimum depth of water	2m 30

Km
Mark Locks

RIVER MAIN

MAINZ
(Connect Route 8)

1

5   **HOCHHEIM.** A famous wine village from which the German white wine known to us as hock became so named.

9   **RUSSELSHEIM**

2

25   **FRANKFURT.** Once the centre for the election and coronation of the German Emperors and today a commercial metropolis of world rank, Frankfurt has a wealth of interesting places to see and of treasures to be discovered. Do not be put off by the industrial approach for a delightful quayside awaits you; which you will find if you use the prominent brownish tower and spire of the cathedral as a leading mark to aim for. When you come near to it you will come to convenient quays by (but not on of course) the line of pleasure boat quays. From here you can step ashore into the interesting old town. Just past the cathedral is 'Die Zeil', one of the best known shopping streets in Europe.
Cathedral 14thC.
Goethe's House and Goethe Museum.
Many museums, Zoo, Tropical Garden.

1

39   **OFFENBACH.** Now a suburb of Frankfurt but a city in its own right with a long history. One of the best known features is the Leather Museum, probably the only one in the world. Here you can see the history of the handbag, Napoleon's briefcase and the toy elephant of Louis XV.

2

Frankfurt.

Km Mark	Locks	Route 12

RIVER MAIN   56   **HANAU.** The Grimm brothers of fairy-tale fame
(From L. River   were born here and a monument in the market
Kinzig)   square records this. It is an interesting town of
half-timbered houses.

         4

87   **ASCHAFFENBURG.** A city of beautiful parks. The
vast Renaissance palace of red sandstone, the
Schloss Johannisburg that you see alongside the
river, stands today as it was in the 17thC; the
marvel is that what stood there in the 17thC was
completely destroyed in WW2.

         2

104   **OBERNBURG**

110   **WORTH.** There is quite a lot of shipping activity
here.

         2

124   **MILTENBURG.** A most attractive village in a
wooded setting.

         2

(From R. River   157   **WERTHEIM.** A pleasant town of half-timbered
Tauber)   houses, beautifully situated in the valley of the
Tauber.

         2

RIVER MAIN   179   **MARKTHEIDENFELD.** A pleasant village.

         1

198   **LOHR.** There is a commercial quay here.

         2

226   **KARLSTADT.** A beautiful town.

         3

252   **WÜRZBURG.** From the river you get the best view
of one of the main attractions of Würzburg, the
fortress, or Festung Marienberg, 12thC.
Situated amidst vineyards Würzburg is an attractive
place. As you may know, Steinwein is the name
frequently used for all Franconian wines, (the only
German wine that does not appear in the flute
bottle). Stein is a famous vineyard of the city of
Würzburg and is in the city above the harbour. The
other famous Würzburg wine name is Leiste.

         4

RIVER MAIN   287   **KITZINGEN**

294   **DETTELBACH**

         4

338   **SCHWEINFURT**

         1

361   **HASSFURT**

         3

Km Mark	*Locks*	**Route 12**

(L. River Main)
(R. River Regnitz)

392   **BAMBERG.** A beautiful cathedral city with water-way interest for two arms of the River Regnitz flow through the centre; but care and attention to the echo sounder is necessary.

CONTINUE AS MAIN-DONAU-KANAL   0

5

44   **ERLANGEN.** A university town and birthplace of Ohm, electrically immortal.

1

Würzburg.

Km Mark	*Locks*	
		Route 12

MAIN-DONAU KANAL

62		**FÜRTH**
	1	
67		**NÜRNBERG (NUREMBERG).** Second city of Bavaria, Nürnberg was one of the most beautiful medieval cities of Germany but much was destroyed during WW2.

Birthplace of Albrecht Dürer, the city is noted for its inventiveness and the originality of its sons.

| | 1 | |
| 72 | | **HAFEN NÜRNBERG** |

Erlangen.

Bamberg . . . The Regnitz. Watch your echo sounder.

The Deutscher Kanal-und Schiffahrtsverein Rhein-Main-Donau e.V. has been committed for more than ninety years to linking the divergent rivers Rhine and Danube. This goal is now near at hand, and this chapter is a tribute to this vast and historical enterprise.

The German-Bavarian link that makes

THE RHINE-MAIN-DANUBE WATERWAY

Within a few years time you will be able to cruise the 3500 kms from the North Sea to the Black Sea, thanks to the efforts of the Federal Republic of Germany and the State of Bavaria in linking up the Rivers Main and Danube.

This waterway link, the connecting of the Rhine, Main and Danube river systems, has been a dream for a thousand years. Charlemagne launched the first project of linking the two rivers by a 2,000 metre long canal; the work, that started in 793, could not be completed owing to adverse weather conditions and military considerations. What is known as "Charlemagne's ditch", the Fossa Carolina at Graben, Weissenburg, is a reminder today of that first effort to link the Rhine and Danube.

King Ludwig I, of Bavaria, was the first to have such a linking canal built and completed, about 150 years ago. It was limited to vessels of 32 m LOA and a beam of 4 m 45, with a full load capacity of 120 tons, and between Bamberg and Kelheim. The horse-drawn vessels of the canal failed to compete with the newly emerging railway systems and thus the canal declined; but the Ludwig Canal was still used by shipping up to the nineteen forties. Just after the turn of the century Donald Maxwell, in *Walrus*, made the through voyage by utilising Ludwig's Canal which, as he said, "brought Holland within rowing distance of the Black Sea". It remains a relic of a byegone age.

On the 6th November 1892, the German Canal and Shipping Association was founded in Nuremberg, its members including 29 cities, 13 chambers of commerce and 286 firms and individuals, with the proposal to link the divergent rivers, Rhine and Danube.

From those beginnings, the new waterway reaching completion in the next five years, is to accomodate the 'Europe Ships' with a cargo capacity of 1,350 tonnes, also of large motor cargo vessels and two unit pushers with dimensions up to 11 m 4 beam and 185 m length and a cargo capacity of 3,300 tonnes; and such craft will be able to cruise through the whole waterway system. In fact, the intention of the new waterway is to bring about the linking of up to 13 European countries along the courses of the Rhine, Main and Danube, (Holland, Belgium, France, Luxembourg, Switzerland, West Germany, Austria, Czechoslovakia, Hungary, Yugoslavia, Rumania, Bulgaria and the Soviet Union).

The cruising yachtsman may wonder if he will be welcome at the lower Danube end of the waterway and whether this will depend more upon political than nautical considerations at least, there are holiday ships, (organised by P & O) regularly cruising the Danube through parts of Hungary and Czechoslovakia; these ships issue the necessary visas to cover approved shore excursions.

The Danube, (or Donau), as you probably know, rises in the Black Forest of West Germany and flows across Austria; it then forms a border between Czechoslovakia and Hungary and flows on into Yugoslavia, forming part borders with that country and Rumania, continuing across Rumania to enter the Black Sea.

The present project was actually set up as long ago as 1921, when the Rhine-Main-Danube Corporation, (RMD), was established with a capital stock of DM200. Under agreements between the then German Reich and the Free State of Bavaria, RMD was simultaneously granted the right to exploit the hydro power of the Aschaffenburg-Bamberg stretch of the Main, the Bavarian Danube, the Altmuhl, the Regnitz and the lower Lech. Construction of the new link was planned to include the building and operating of hydro power plants on the rivers to be canalized. The capital costs of the whole project were to be recovered from earnings from the power plants. By the 1950s, construction of the overall project was well under way, with the Kachlet-Stufe power plant on the Danube, (one of the biggest in the world), and the canalization of the River Main.

THE MAIN-DANUBE WATERWAY

The total length of the Main-Danube waterway, from Aschaffenburg to Passau, (the national border), is 677 km. This includes the 297 km stretch of the Main between Aschaffenburg and Bamberg, the 171 km Main-Danube canal between Bamberg and

Main-Danube Waterway
Longitudinal Section

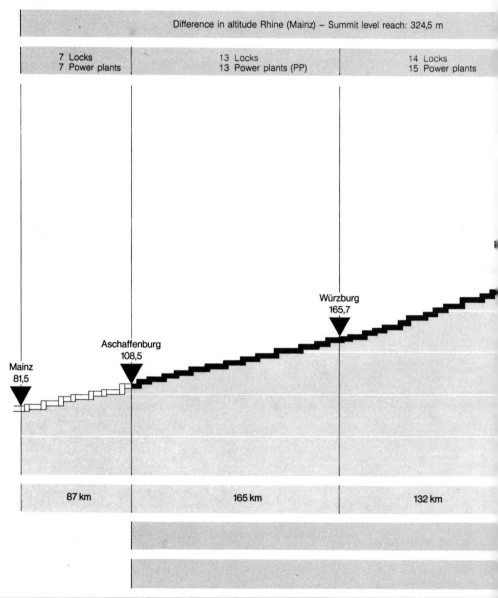

Difference in altitude Rhine (Mainz) – Summit level reach: 324,5 m

7 Locks
7 Power plants

13 Locks
13 Power plants (PP)

14 Locks
15 Power plants

Würzburg
165,7

Aschaffenburg
108,5

Mainz
81,5

87 km

165 km

132 km

Main
km
0

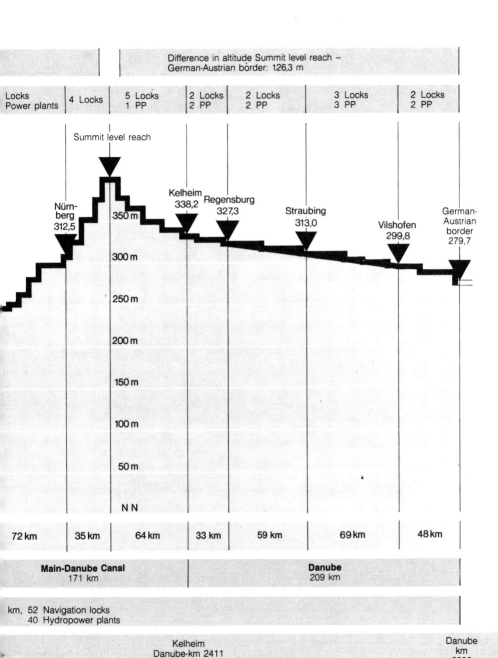

Locks Power plants	4 Locks	5 Locks 1 PP	2 Locks 2 PP	2 Locks 2 PP	3 Locks 3 PP	2 Locks 2 PP

Difference in altitude Summit level reach – German-Austrian border: 126,3 m

Summit level reach

Nürnberg 312,5

350 m

Kelheim 338,2

Regensburg 327,3

Straubing 313,0

Vilshofen 299,8

German-Austrian border 279,7

300 m
250 m
200 m
150 m
100 m
50 m
N N

72 km	35 km	64 km	33 km	59 km	69 km	48 km

Main-Danube Canal 171 km　　　　　**Danube** 209 km

km, 52 Navigation locks
　　40 Hydropower plants

Kelheim
Danube-km 2411
MDC-km 171

Danube
km
2202

Kelheim, and the 209 km Danube part between Kelheim and the Austrian frontier.

In comparison to the Ludwig Canal, the new RMD waterway was intended to be integrated in the overall European waterway system from the beginning; and this beginning was the canalizing of the Main and Danube.

CANALIZATION OF THE MAIN

The Main was canalized from Aschaffenburg to Bamberg between 1926 and 1962, a distance of 297 km with 27 locks having an aggregate lift of 122 m. The channel still has to be deepened to 3 m between Aschaffenburg and Wurtzburg, and some bend radii increased.

CANALIZATION OF THE DANUBE

In the 1920s the Kachlet barrage was built above Passau; in the 1950s the Jochenstein barrage at the national frontier was built in cooperation with Austria. The channel depth has been improved between Kelheim and Regensburg by the construction of groins and training works. In 1978 the stretch between Kelheim and Regensburg was opened, increasing the navigable section of the Danube to 209 km. In the Regensburg-Straubing section, two barrages, at Geisling and Straubing, are under construction.

CONSTRUCTION OF THE BAMBERG-KELHEIM STRETCH

The 72 km section of the Main-Danube, following the Regnitz valley from Bamberg to Nuremburg, was completed between 1960 and 1972, negotiating a level difference of 82 m with seven locks. Nuremburg has, of course, been the dead end port of the northern section of the Main-Danube waterway. The work remaining to be completed is the 99 km southern section from Nuremburg to Kelheim, consisting of a 26 km northern ramp, with four locks overcoming a level difference of 93 m 5, and reaching the summit at Hilpoltstein. The two locks at Eibach and Leerstetten are finished and the other two are under construction. With lifts of up to 24 m 7 they rate amongst the highest shaft locks with water-saving side ponds.

The summit is 406 m above sea level, crossing the Jura which is the watershed between the Rhine and the Danube. Descending to the

Danube will be three locks of 170 m 0 lift each. Near Dietfurt, the canal joins the River Altmuhl which will be canalized for 34 km, then flowing into the Danube at Kelheim.

Out of the 99 km remaining, 43 km have been completed and another 14 km are under construction. Four of the nine locks are completed and three are being built.

The work entailed in digging the Main-Danube Canal had to be deferred until the rivers, (which it was to connect), were dredged and made navigable for year round operation. The biggest job, on the Main, involved channeling the river and building 27 locks from Aschaffenburg to Bamberg.

In scheming to carry the waterway over hills and valleys and roads, the engineers were not automatically in favour of locks, in view of their expense and slowing of traffic; they devised a waterway fly-over spanning the Rednitz river valley, a suspended trough containing nearly 1 million cubic feet of water.

Where lock type systems had to be considered, the merits of barge lifts on the north and south ramps of the summit reach were considered; but after much further consideration, preference was given to the construction of staircase locks. Accordingly, at Leerstetten, Eckersmuhlen and Hilpoltstein there are three locks, each with a lift of 24 m 7.

To give you an idea of the total number of locks you might have to contemplate in the various sections of the whole waterway between Mainz on the Main, (Rhine junction), and the German-Austrian border on the Danube, I have prepared the following small table:—

River/ Canal	From	Alt	To	Alt	Kms	No. of locks
Main	Mainz	81.5	Aschaffenburg	108.5	87	7
,,	Aschaffenburg	108.5	Wurzburg	165.7	165	13
,,	Wurzburg	165.7	Bamberg	230.8	132	14
Main/	Bamberg	230.8	Nurnberg	312.5	72	5
Donau/	Nurnberg	312.5	Summit	406.0	35	4
Canal	Summit	406.0	Kelheim	338.2	64	5
Danube	Kelheim	338.2	Regensberg	327.3	33	2
,,	Regensberg	327.3	Straubing	313.0	59	2
,,	Straubing	313.0	Vilshofen	229.8	69	3
,,	Vilshofen	299.8	Frontier	279.7	48	2

Since the total amount of work has extended over a period of sixty years, the various sections and locks were constructed in accordance with the size and type of vessel in use at the time. At the outset, locks of some length were built to accommodate towed trains of barges; later, with self-propelled craft and pushers, wider locks became necessary. As mentioned above, the Main-Donau-Canal and the Kelheim-Regensburg Section of the Danube, are being developed to the standards of Waterway Category IV.

The result of this vast enterprise will be a rapid rise in European inter-nation trade, since water transport is acknowledged to be a most economical method of carrying bulk freight. There is expected to be a considerable increase in river traffic and tourism too, since the waterway passes through some of the most picturesque areas of Europe.

Although the waterway will not be completely opened up for another five years, the economic benefits are already being felt. Despite the fact that Nuremberg is 750 km from the nearest sea it is already thriving as an inland port. Other ports are quoting dramatic increases in trade.

The completed waterway will stimulate trade over a wide area. And as for the leisure aspect, imagine cruising in your yacht from Rotterdam to the Black Sea.

Kelheim Reach – near Altessing.

When the Rhein-Main-Donau Waterway is complete, it will be possible for us, cruising from the north-west, to explore the Danube towards its source, turning right at Kelheim instead of continuing straight on towards the Black Sea. This has always been possible, of course, for craft coming 'up' the Danube from the south-east.

Rising in the Alps, close to the Rhine, the Danube flows east to the Black Sea. One might say that navigation begins at Ulm, although you will find boats beyond this.

From Ulm to Kelheim (where the Danube carries on but will, from this point, be the Rhein-Main-Donau Waterway), a good deal of canalization has been carried out and there are nineteen locks of international standard.

Route 13 **Mannheim to Plochingen**

Distance	197 kms
Number of locks	26
Minimum height above water	2m 10
Minimum depth of water	2m 30

Kms Locks

RIVER NECKAR   **MANNHEIM**
(Connect Route 8)

　　　　　　1

13   **LADENBURG.** An ancient town of attractive
timbered houses, founded by the Romans and with
well preserved town fortifications.

　　　　　　1

10   **HEIDELBERG.** The best views of this centre of
Heidelberg.

	Kms	Locks	Route 13

RIVER NECKAR — German Romanticism are from the river; the red walls of the castle against the green of the forest are almost too beautiful to be real and you think of a stage set. On theatrical lines the university of Heidelberg, oldest in Germany, was the setting for The Student Prince.

Heidelberg has been much praised in word and song and the fascinating old town is near to your mooring for there is a selection of convenient quay walls here.

5 / I — **ZIEGELHAUSEN.** A small resort.

(R. River Elsenz) 6 / I — **NECKAR-GEMUND.** A small health resort at the mouth of the River Elsenz.

4 — **NECKAR-STEINACH.** Noted for its four castles. If you stop by the small quay leave room for the Dilsberg ferry.

9 / I — **HIRSCHHORN.** A beautiful place of medieval buildings and, of course, with a castle, also a 15thC Gothic church.

11 / I — **EBERBACH.** A most attractive health resort. The tree lined hills sweep right down from the Odenwald, almost to the quay.

22 / 2 — **MOSBACH.** A small town of elegant timbered houses.

13 / I — **GUNDELSHEIM.** There are more castles in view here. Above the town is Castle Horneck.

(L. River Jagst) *(L. River Kocher)* 6 / I — **BAD WIMPFEN.** A beautiful town and health resort. There was once a Roman citadel here.

3 — **BAD FRIEDRICHSHALL**

3 / I — **NECKARSULM.** The NSU factory is here and in the old castle is the German Motorcycle Museum.

7 — **HEILBRONN.** A pleasant town in vineyard country with quite a big harbour. Heilbronn has been rebuilt since December 1944 when it was destroyed by bombing.

There is industry here, also a famous Town Hall clock. The most famous sons of Heilbronn are Mayer, (conservation of energy), Maybach, (inventor of the carburettor) and Mauser, (guns).

Kms	*Locks*

RIVER NECKAR

(R. River Enz)

4

24   **BESIGHEIM.** An attractive old town between the Neckar and Enz rivers. You see vineyards everywhere and some quite notable wines are produced here.

2

18   **MARBACH.** Schiller was born here and the huge castle-like building above the valley is the Schiller National Museum.

5

29   **STUTTGART.** The star of Mercedes lights up the sky over this modern and original city. Gottlieb Daimler lived in Bad Cannstatt and put the Mercedes car on the market at the turn of the century. The Daimler-Benz Automobile Museum is still in the Bad Canstatt area, in Mercedesstrasse, in which area there is also a lock and a convenient place to moor.

In the museum are details of the aeroplanes, cars, railways and ships powered by the firms' engines and a fascinating section on the racing history of

Stuttgart.

Kms Locks **Route 13**

RIVER NECKAR

Mercedes cars with a collection of racing cars from the first days of motor sports to the present. There are other museums and art galleries, theatres, a hill composed of debris of WW2 and the Television Tower, 712ft high with the observation platform and restaurant at 492ft.

14   4   **PLOCHINGEN**

Poppenweiler lock.

Route 14 **Travemünde to Lauenburg**

Distance	72 kms
Number of locks	8
Minimum height above water	4m 20
Minimum depth of water	2m

RIVER TRAVE

TRAVEMÜNDE. There is a pleasant harbour with easy mooring in this popular seaside resort at the mouth of the River Trave; it is a popular holiday area for all around the coast from here to the Kieler Förde and above you see camping and caravan sites everywhere. The Customs quay is to port on entry and the Polizei are on the other side, just inland. The PASSATHAFEN is the yacht harbour.

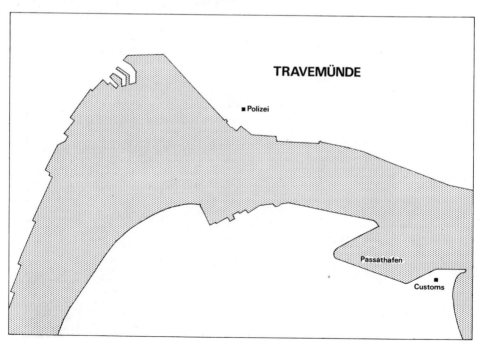

	Kms	**Route 14**

RIVER TRAVE

Travemünde, with its flourishing casino, is the focal point of the holiday activity of the area. It is also a ferry terminal for Finland and Sweden, the ferries for Denmark using the port of Puttgarden on what was the island of Fehmarn but is now connected by a bridge to the mainland.

The shipyard at Travemünde builds yachts of the utmost luxury.

Cruising outside of Travemünde in the Lübecher Bucht you have to be careful to keep to 'your side' of the buoyed channel and not to stray into the waters of the People's Republic.

15

LÜBECK. Although it is principally an industrial town the spires seem to outnumber the chimneys as you approach and the green of grass and trees alongside the river make a greater impression than the factories. All the prominent buildings are built of red brick for which Lübeck is famous; it is also famous as the 'Queen of Hansa' for it was the capital of the Hanseatic League. The fine old buildings around the harbour and in the centre of the town give an indication of its former prosperity and there is no problem in finding a berth alongside some pleasant quay. The town is ringed with canals.

RIVER TRAVE

On approach you will probably find it most convenient to make for the Hansahafen and when proceeding on your way inland you will turn back

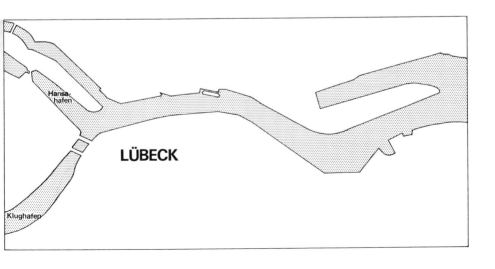

		Kms	*Locks*	

Kms Locks   **Route 14**

Lubeck (cont.)

into the Klughafen. Holstentor fortified gate 15thC.
Town Hall from 13thC.
St. Mary's church, Gothic brick, 14thC.

(R. Obere Trave)   5
CONTINUE AS
ELBE-LÜBECK
    KANAL   29   **MOLLN.** In the Middle Ages this was an important
place when the salt trade from Lauenburg to
Lübeck flourished.

     15   **BÜCHEN.** From here the border runs close again
and the malevolent watch-towers cast their depressing
spell. So much so that the foredeckhand produced a
bottle of Schloss Reinhartshausener to toast our
good fortune at being the right side of the grim
wire.

        3
     13   **LAUENBURG**
(Connect Routes 3, 10)

Route 15 **Uffeln to Ruhen**

Distance	271 kms
Number of locks	2
Minimum height above water	4m
Minimum depth of water	2m

	Kms	*Locks*	
MITTELLAND KANAL (R. Zweigkanal nach Osnabrüch)	29		**UFFELN**

- -

	Kms	*Locks*	
ZWEIGKANAL NACH OSNABRUCH	14	2	**OSNABRÜCK.** With a cathedral dating back almost a thousand years and a Town Hall in which the Treaty of Westphalia, (which ended the Thirty Years War), was signed. Osnabrück has a place in history. Future historians may record that it is now a big producer of pumpernickel and a manufacturing town.

- -

	Kms	
MITTELLAND KANAL	6	**BRAMSCHE.** There is a small quay here.
	7	**ENGTER**
	24	**BAD ESSEN.** A pretty little health resort with a little industry and an industrial quay.
	12	**GETMOLD**
	8	**LÜBBECKE**
(L. Mittel-Weser) (L. Mittel-Weser) (R. Ober-Weser) (R. Ober-Weser)	20	**MINDEN.** The Mittelland Kanal passes over the River Weser here, a unique situation. Minden is a pleasant little place with a commercial harbour and an industrial scene hidden, or softened, by green

Kms

Route 15

MITTELLAND
KANAL

spaces and parks. The deep Minden lock is a place of entertainment as well as a mover of canal traffic and as you carry out your expert lock drill you will be gratified to learn that the spectators behind the railings have paid to watch you.
(Connect Route 16)

33   **SACHSENHAGEN**

LEFT FORK
(Str. on Zweigkanal
nach Hannover-Linden)
(L. Leine)

33   **HANNOVER.** Less than three hundred years after the Elector George left Hannover to become King George I of England the planes of his

Hannover.

	Kms	*Locks*	**Route 15**

MITTELLAND
KANAL

successor, George VI, were busy destroying it. Practically nothing was left of the old town but a great deal of reconstruction has taken place. Our route on the Mittelland Kanal passes through the northern part of Hannover whereas the diversion on the River Leine takes you almost alongside the Herrenhäusen Gardens, started in the 17thC and now one of the most beautiful parks in Europe. Hannover is best known today, probably, for its Industrial Fair, an event of world importance. It is a lively and industrious city with elegant shopping areas. There are several museums and a zoo.

(L. to Misburg)

          I

(R. Zweigkanal nach 12
Hildesheim)

- -

ZWEIGKANAL   I
NACH HILDESHEIM 14

HILDESHEIM. Although many buildings were destroyed in WW2 a great deal of rebuilding has been carried out in this one time centre of the medieval Saxon and Salian Kings. Some of the fine old houses of the Brühl quarter escaped damage.

- -

MITTELLAND 17
KANAL
(R. Zweigkanal nach 14
Salzgitter)

PEINE

    22

BRAUNSCHWEIG (BRUNSWICK). The harbour is on the Mittelland Kanal but the town is not, although it is not far away. It is the second largest town of Lower Saxony and although in an area known as a vegetable garden Brunswick is an industrial town. It is also the town of Henry the Lion who married the daughter of Henry II Plantagenet.

          I

    22

WOLFSBURG

    12

RUHEN

Route 16 **Verden to Kassel**

Distance 333 kms
Number of locks 14
Minimum height above water 4m
Minimum depth of water 1m 35

Kms Locks

RIVER ALLER

VERDEN. A pleasant place with an interesting Horse Museum and a fine cathedral. It is a horse loving, riding and racing area.
(Connect Route 1)

*LEFT INTO
MITTEL-WESER*

1

24 **HOYA.** There are pleasant moorings here.

1

31 **NIENBURG.** A market town with attractive gabled houses, a square and a quay.

10 **LIEBENAU**

1

11 **STOLZENAU**

1

. . . the Weser
near Stolzenau.

	Kms	*Locks*	**Route 16**
MITTEL-WESER	19		**PETERSHAGEN**
LEFT FORK		1	
	24		**MINDEN**
			(Connect Route 15)
CONTINUE AS			
OBER-WESER	22		**VLOTHO.** Quite a pleasant village.
	15		**RINTELN.** A cheerful little place with a harbour.
	29		**HAMELN (HAMELIN).**

HAMELN (HAMELIN). Going ashore to do the shopping you may wonder at the number of chocolate and confectionery rats in the shop windows until you realise that this is the town of the Pied Piper and a charming town of fine 17thC

... the Pied Piper.

Kms	Locks	Route 16

OBER-WESER — houses it is. If you are here on a Sunday you can see the drama of the Pied Piper enacted with the Piper in his medieval clothes and children dressed as rats doing the Rat Dance.
Ratcatchers House 17thC.

1

23 — **BODENWERDER.** Has a small harbour.

32 — **HÖXTER.** An old Hansa town with unusual half timbered houses, gaily decorated and painted.

19 — **BEVERUNGEN**

14 — **KARLSHAFEN.** An attractive town with a pleasant quay.

32 — **HANNOVERSCH MÜNDEN.** An old town of splendid timbered houses at the junction of the rivers Fulda and Werra.

CONTINUE AS RIVER FULDA

7

27 — **KASSEL.** A big industrial centre with an industrial harbour but with many attractions for visitors. There are fine parks and an art gallery with one of the finest collections in Germany. There are several museums, one of them, the Brothers Grimm Museum, recalls the brothers' twenty-five years work here. Wilhelmshöhe Castle; Löwenburg Castle.

1

The RIVER FULDA continues south as a CLASS 0 waterway through

MELSUNGEN, a town of half-timbered houses and

BEBRA to

MECKLAR

Route 17 **Wesel to Hamm**

Distance	73 kms
Number of locks	8
Minimum height above water	4m
Minimum depth of water	2m 50

	Kms	Locks	
WESEL-DATTELN- *KANAL*			**WESEL** *(Connect Route 11)*
		3	
	28		**DORSTEN.** An industrial town with an industrial harbour.
		3	
(From L. Dortmund- *Ems Kanal)* *RIGHT, RHEIN-* *HERNE-KANAL*			**DATTELN** *(Connect Route 6)*
LEFT, DATTELN- *HAMM-KANAL*			
	15		**LÜNEN**
	15		**WERNE**
		1	
	15		**HAMM.** An industrial town. South of Hamm is Soest, below which, on the Ruhr river, is the Möhne Dam that you may remember.
		1	

Route 18 **Wilhelmshaven to Emden**

Distance	71 kms
Number of locks	6
Minimum height above water	unlimited
Minimum depth of water	1m 40

EMS-JADE KANAL

(L. Nordgeorgsfehn-kanal)

WILHELMSHAVEN. Situated on the Jadebusen, or Jade Bay, once the most important naval port of Germany and destroyed in WW2, Wilhelmshaven is now growing in importance as an oil port with an oil pipeline extending 400kms to the Ruhr basin. There are beaches and mud baths—enough mud to bath the population is on this coast—and trips to the Frisian islands and an aquarium, all calculated to entice holidaymakers to this otherwise doleful place.
The harbour is industrial but not crowded. Once through the sea-lock you can usually pick your spot, or about 2 miles further on, (from seaward) and

Pontonhaven near Wilhelmshaven.

Kms *Locks* **Route 18**

EMS-JADE KANAL

round the corner to starboard is the Pontonhafen (see photo), in more of a yachting environment.

4

42 **AURICH.** There is quite a pleasant little harbour here.

2

29 **EMDEN.** As passage through the bridges allows, proceed towards the Rathaus as your landmark to secure the best berth.

(Connect Route 6)

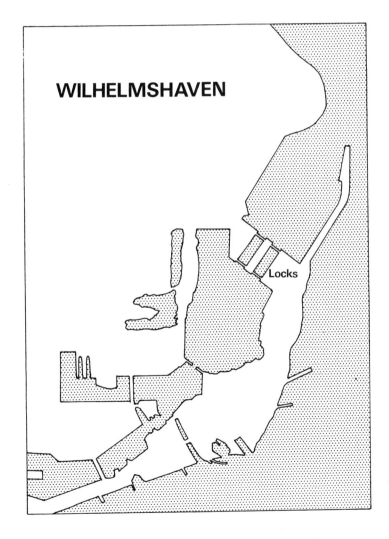

WILHELMSHAVEN

Locks

From Holland into Germany

Route HG/1 Delfzijl to Emden

Distance	18 kms
Number of locks	2
Minimum height above water	unlimited
Minimum depth of water	2m

	Kms	Locks	
RIVER EMS		1	**DELFZIJL**
	18	1	**EMDEN**
			(Connect Routes 6, 18)

Route HG/2 Ter Apel to Haren

Distance	18 kms
Number of locks	6
Minimum height above water	unlimited
Minimum depth of water	2m

	Kms	
STADS COMPASCUUM KANAL		**TER APEL**
	1	
	5	**FRONTIER**
HAREN-RÜTEN KANAL	1	**RÜTENBROCK**
	5	
DORTMUND-EMS KANAL	12	**HAREN**
		(Connect Route 6)

Route HG/3 **Coevorden to Lingen (near)**

Distance		55 kms
Number of locks		7
Minimum height above water		6m
Minimum depth of water		1m 70

	Kms	Locks		
COEVORDEN-PICCARDIE KANAL			**COEVORDEN**	*A permit may be required.
	5		**FRONTIER**	
	16	4	**GEORGSDORF**	
RIGHT, SUD-NORD KANAL				
	17	3	**NORDHORN**	
LEFT, EMS-VECHT KANAL				
RIVER EMS	17		**LINGEN** (near) *(Connect Route 6)*	

Route HG/4 **Lobith to Emmerich**

Distance		11 kms
Number of locks		0
Minimum height above water		unlimited
Minimum depth of water		2m 50

RIVER RHEIN		**LOBITH**
(R. Spoykanal, 10kms to Kleve where there is a harbour; 1 lock depth 2m headroom unlimited)	2	**FRONTIER**
	9	**EMMERICH** *(Connect Route 9)*

From France into Germany

Route FG/1 **Thionville to Perl**

Distance	25 kms
Number of locks	2
Minimum height above water	3m 70
Minimum depth of water	2m 60

	Kms	Locks	
RIVER MOSELLE			**THIONVILLE**
		1	
	23		**FRONTIER**
		1	
	2		**PERL**
			(Connect Route 9)

The Moselle is the frontier between Germany and Luxembourg from Perl to the River Sûre.

Route FG/2 **Strasbourg to Lauterbourg**

Distance	61 kms
Number of locks	1
Minimum height above water	7m
Minimum depth of water	2m 70

	Kms	Locks	
RIVER RHEIN			**STRASBOURG**
		1	
	20		**DRUSENHEIM**
	20		**SELTZ**
	21		**LAUTERBOURG**

The River Rhein forms the frontier between France and Germany for 200kms, from the Swiss frontier at Basle to Lauterbourg.

9 Useful addresses

A brochure containing all the river signs, navigational directions, lights and signals that you may need during your German cruise, can be obtained free of charge by writing to:—

ADAC
Am Westpark 8,
8000 Munchen 70,
West Germany.

Rules, regulations and one way navigation systems may vary, if only slightly, from one waterway authority to another. It is advisable to check with the regional shipping and yachting authorities responsible for the waterway you intend to cruise. They are:—

ELBE AND THE KIEL CANAL:—
Wasser-und Schiffahrtsdirektion Nord,
Hindenburgufer 247,
D–2300 KIEL.

EMS AND WESER (NORTHERN PART)
Wasser-und Schiffahrtsdirektion Nordwest,
Schlossplatz 9, D–2960 AURICH.

EDER, WESER (CENTRAL PART)
Wasser-und Schiffahrtsdirektion Mitte,
Am Waterlooplatz 5,
D–3000 HANNOVER.

RHINE (Northern half)
Wasser-und Schiffahrtsdirektion West,
Cheruskerring 11,
D–440 MUNSTER.

NECKAR, MAIN, LAIN, MOSEL, SAAR AND THE
SOUTHERN HALF OF THE RHINE.
Wasser-und Schiffahrtsdirektion Sudwest,
Stresemannufer 2,
D–6500 MAINZ.

MAIN, MAIN-DANUBE-KANAL, DANUBE
Wasser-und Schiffahrtsdirektion Sud,
Worthstrasse 19,
D–8700 WURZBURG.

Index

Note: An index of PLACE NAMES
appears on page 63
An index of WATERWAYS
appears on page 66